VINTAGE BARGETTO

Celebrating a Century of California Winemaking

John E. Bargetto

Geoffrey Dunn

Afterword by Sandy Lydon

Dedication

John E. Bargetto

As a young boy, I always enjoyed hearing stories. And the best ones were from my parents, aunts and uncles, brothers and sisters, cousins, winery employees, and from the church, too. Through these innumerable stories, I believe that I developed an appreciation of history at a young age.

My mother, Beverly Regan Bargetto, was the family historian of her generation. And thank God for that! For without her own story-telling and devotion to history by keeping documents, photos, 8-mm film, I fear how much of our family and winery history would have been lost forever.

It is my privilege to dedicate this book to my loving mother Beverly—to whom I owe so infinitely more than I could ever honor in a single book.

Easter, March 31, 2013

During the early 1960s, my family relocated from westside Santa Cruz to the fertile Soquel Valley of Central California, less than a mile above the distinctive brick-colored barn that housed Bargetto Winery. Soquel was a small and quiet community at the time, slowly emerging from its rural roots into a suburb of Santa Cruz and, later, a bedroom community for Silicon Valley.

As it turned out, my mother's extended family—she was a member of the Stagnaro fishing clan on the Santa Cruz waterfront—had many longtime friendships and even business relationships with the Bargetto family dating back generations. It was an important social link. Before long I counted several of the Bargetto cousins among my friends as well.

Our families are from nearby regions of Italy—Piemonte and Liguria, respectively—and I immediately recognized many of the same traits on the Bargetto family compound (the importance of family, a love of food and wine and intense conversation) that I had experienced in my own close-knit Italian family in Santa Cruz. So it was that Bargetto Winery became something of a talisman in my youth, a geographical touchstone if you will, and has remained one all of my life.

While I have always been an aficionado of Bargetto wines and have been equally fascinated by the family's ever-growing winery, what I remember most—and respect profoundly to this day—were the strong family ties that bound this remarkable clan together over the decades. I feel uniquely fortunate to have counted many of them as friends for nearly a half-century (we are aging like good, vintage wine) and blessed to have been introduced to yet another bright and talented generation of the family. It has been an honor to have worked with members of the family, and in particular the family historian, John Bargetto, on this special centennial project.

Four generations of Bargettos have now graced the Soquel Valley. Soon, I am sure, there will be a fifth. All of the elders who guided the family compound when I was a boy have now passed, but their legacy is enduring. Theirs is a rich, colorful and iconic American story.

Foreword

The Bargetto Family in Soquel: An Iconic American Story

Geoffrey Dunn, Ph. D.
June 2013

Contents

Vineyards in the Asti area of Piemonte, Italy.

Acknowledgments

John E. Bargetto

Writing a book may seem like a not-so-daunting task...until one begins to write. And then one realizes it is nearly an impossible endeavor, and, perhaps, like whale hunting, the "animal" just gets bigger and bigger. Once in the middle of the project, you realize it cannot be finished without the help of many people.

I would like to start by thanking all my family members, both past and present, who have devoted their lives to establish and sustain our family winery. It is only because of their vision and perseverance that I have something to write about. I also am grateful to the generations of employees, most of whom are too numerous to mention, who have toiled for the past century. These dedicated employees have worked in the vineyard, in the laboratory, in the cellars, in retail operations and in administration. Because of their devotion, our long-standing family tradition is alive and well.

Specific to the book, I especially thank those who encouraged me in the early stages. There was plenty of time at the beginning of the book when I would ask... "Is there a book here?" The real early co-visionaries were Edward Penniman, book designer, and Geoffrey Dunn, co-author. Ed, with his artistic flair and wonderful patience, designed each page beautifully. Geoffrey brought his research and writing experience and was a great asset in finding images, especially for the early chapters. Without their support and encouragement, this book would have remained just a dream.

I am indebted to cousin Tom Bargetto, who painstakingly helped me edit every chapter, improved historical accuracy, and, from his mother's teaching, helped to improve grammar. I wish to thank our British-born winemaker Michael Sones for his own appreciation of history, and for encouraging me to forge ahead with the project.

I am grateful to all of my many editors, both official and unofficial, who gave me encouragement and vastly improved the book. The official editors include the following: sisters Loretta and Donna, brothers Martin and Richard, daughter Gianna, Geoffrey Dunn and Siri Vaeth-Dunn. I am grateful to historian Charles Sullivan for reviewing the Santa Cruz Mountains history section in chapter two.

And to my wife Sharon, daughters Gianna and Elisa and son Kevin, I thank them for giving me the time and space for the book, and for listening to all the daily adventures (and occasional frustrations) involved. For any errors or omissions, I alone take full responsibility.

Introduction

John E. Bargetto

To say that Italians like to talk is, of course, an understatement. Yet through communication at mealtimes and other family gatherings, vital familial stories are passed down from one generation to the next in the oral tradition. This is true in the Bargetto family as well, where some of the best stories have only been kept alive because of this story-telling tradition. In our case, someone was willing to take the time to tell a story and others were willing to listen. (Perhaps our information-age society could benefit from a bit more of this time-honored practice.) I believe in the art of communication, particularly in person. My experience has been that through oral tradition, not only have I learned family and winery history, but also I have developed emotional connections with our family.

This book will, for the first time, record the unique history of Bargetto Winery and the Bargetto family, intermixing documented historical research with occasional family lore.

I am the self-described family historian of my generation. As a very shy young man, it was easy for me to simply listen to the older generation tell their stories. Now, their stories are our stories. The story tellers of the previous generation were Auntie Sylvia and Auntie Adeline (double first cousins to my father), my father Lawrence and Auntie Micky. Beverly Bargetto, my mother, not only enthusiastically shared her interest in the winery and family history, but also kept all sorts of records and photos. But no one in the family was better at telling the family wine stories than Uncle Ralph. My generation owes him a debt of gratitude for being such a great raconteur, and for keeping the family stories alive.

In college, when I studied Enology (winemaking) at the University of California, Davis, I decided to balance my scientific studies with history classes. I completed a minor in European Cultural History. Later I realized that I was brought up, to some degree, actually living European culture. I enjoyed the history classes thoroughly and often found them to be a welcome break from studying biochemistry and wine phenolics. I did raise a few eyebrows with my classmates when I told them I was off on my bike to a history class.

When I returned from my graduate studies to re-join the family business, all I had in terms of a written winery history was a four page typed list showing a few dates and key activities. This document chronologically listed birth and death dates of family members and high points of the winery activities, e.g., 1906 Filippo returned to Casa Delmas, or 1934 opened Water Street retail room in Santa Cruz.

There was no description, no detail and no emotion. Aside from some photo albums and scattered photos, this was the limit of our winery history. This limited but vital document was completed by Adeline and Sylvia Bargetto in the 1970s.

About 15 years ago, I decided that it was time for the winery to have an "archive." So in an oversized file cabinet I organized the photos, articles, awards, etc. by decade: pre-1910, 1910, 1920 and so on. This was the next incremental step toward compiling the winery history. In time, as the archives grew, the story began to unfold.

In 2013, Bargetto Winery celebrates its 80th anniversary in Soquel. Yet, with the first family winery opening in San Francisco in 1909, we really are recognizing more than 100 years of California wine-making. With so many of the historical wineries being sold to large conglomerates, Bargetto has now become one of the most historic wineries in the state of California. In fact, out of nearly 4,000 California wineries, there are now fewer than 10 older than Bargetto.

Starting the summer of 2012, I thought that it was time to formally examine, research, compile and write the Bargetto Winery history, and to explore the possibility of a book. Voila! I thank you for showing interest in our own unique wine and family history. I imagine that you might find some similarities to your own family history.

Sit back, have a glass of wine and enjoy our story.

Sincerely,

John E. Bargetto
Winemaker and Bargetto Family Historian

It has become quite a common proverb
that in wine there is truth: [in vino veritas].
—Pliny the Elder

Chapter One

300 Years in Castelnuovo Don Bosco
1680-Present

Like an ancient and gnarled grapevine, the Bargetto family wine story winds its way back to the foothills of the Italian Alps, in what is known as the Piemonte region (Piedmont in English) of northwestern Italy. Of course, the tradition of winemaking in Italy dates back thousands of years, even prior to the Roman Empire. The earliest evidence of winemaking has been discovered by archeologists in the regions of Eastern Europe dating back as far as 7000 B.C.

While Greek and Estruscan influences can be traced to the Italian peninsula stretching back millennia, the Roman Empire had a pivotal influence in the development of wine. Wine production—and consumption—was closely linked to Roman mythology. Bacchus was the Roman god of the grape harvest and wine (in ancient Greece, it was Dionysus), and as early as 500 B.C., wine consumption played an important role in Roman culture and festivities. Perhaps most significantly, wine consumption was eventually viewed as a democratic activity: slaves, peasants and the ruling class alike all drank wine as part of their daily food intake.

During the era of the Roman Empire, agricultural technology improved greatly, as Roman armies spread viticulture to all regions of the empire. In more recent centuries, in what would eventually become modern-day Italy (which was unified formally in 1861), great advances were made in vine cultivation techniques, wine presses and the creation of wooden barrels for aging and shipment. The great Roman writers—from Cato to Ovid to Pliny to Virgil—all referenced either winemaking or wine consumption in their literary endeavors.

Winegrowing in the Piemonte region, which borders both France and Switzerland, dates back centuries. Today, the Piemonte region is world famous for winemaking. It is the home to 45 "Controlled designation of origin" wines known in Italian as *Denominazione di Origine Controllata* (or DOC) and 16 of the highest level of "guaranteed" Italian wines known as *Denominazione di Origine Controllata e Garantita* (or DOCG). In contrast, Tuscany has just six of

The Young Bacchus, c.1589
Caravaggio, Michelangelo Merisi da
(1571-1610),
Galleria degli Uffizi, Florence, Italy.
The Bridgeman Art Library

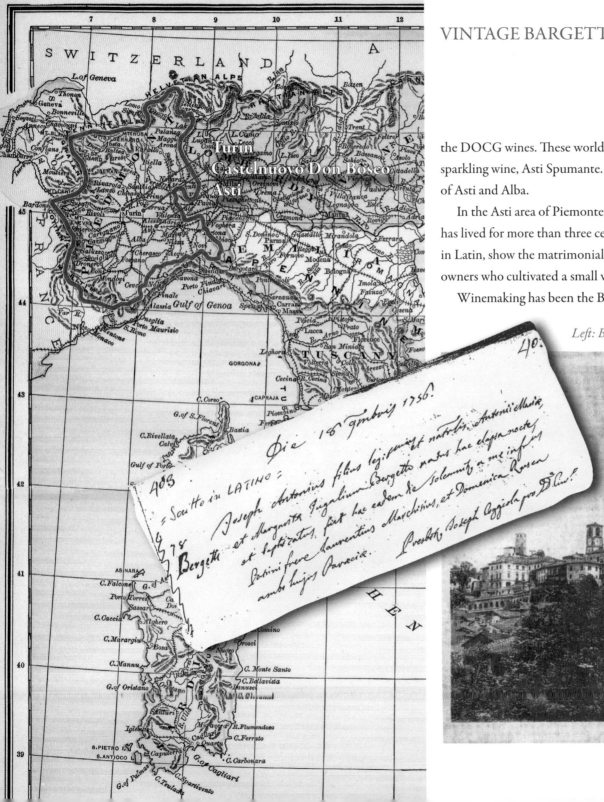

VINTAGE BARGETTO: Celebrating a Century of California Winemaking.

the DOCG wines. These world famous wines include Barolo, Barbaresco, Barbera d'Asti and also the sparkling wine, Asti Spumante. The heart of this region's viticulture industry is centered in the villages of Asti and Alba.

In the Asti area of Piemonte, just 35 miles due north from the town of Barolo, the Bargetto family has lived for more than three centuries. Catholic Church documents from Castelnuovo d'Asti, written in Latin, show the matrimonial lineage dating back to circa 1680. The Bargetto progenitors were landowners who cultivated a small vineyard and developed a family tradition as winemakers in the village.

Winemaking has been the Bargetto lifeblood and has served as their profession for generations. The

Left: Bargetto family marriage church document written in Latin 1756.

Castelnuovo Don Bosco - Panorama

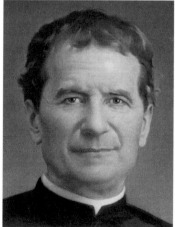

Saint John "Don" Bosco

small hill town of Castelnuovo d'Asti is home to the red Dolcetto grape variety and the white Arneis. Almost certainly these would have been the wines that the Bargetto family produced and sold several centuries ago.

In 1930, the town known as Castelnuovo d'Asti was eventually changed to Castelnuovo Don Bosco, in honor of San Giovanni (John) Bosco. He was born in a log cabin in the hamlet of Becchi, close to Castelnuovo d'Asti in 1815. (In the 1830s he lived in a Bargetto relative's home in the town of Chieri.) Giovanni Bosco came to be known as "Don Bosco" and founded the Salesian Society order of priests and nuns. He was a man who devoted his life to helping orphaned boys in and around Torino (Turin), Italy.

Don Bosco was canonized a saint by Pope Pius XI in 1934. The Salesian Order spread around the world and currently operates 5,000 schools. (Today, the Salesians of Don Bosco operate two schools not far from Bargetto Winery in Santa Cruz County, Salesian Elementary School and St. Francis High School.)

In the beginning of the 19th century, Castelnuovo d'Asti had only a few hundred residents. Thus the Bargetto and Bosco families would have certainly known each other. Giovanni Antonio Bargetto, born in 1820 in Castelnuovo d'Asti, would have grown up with Don Bosco and most likely attended the same church and played in the same town plaza. Giovanni Antonio Bargetto's son, Giuseppe, was the first Bargetto to venture to California later in the 19th century. He and the internationally renowned saint would have been only one generation removed from one another.

Through the well-documented life of Don Bosco, we can gather

Dolcetto grapes, photo courtesy Eric Vogt.

Istituto Salesiano "Bernardi Semeria" eretto presso la Casetta di San Giovanni Bosco.

Right: Giuseppe Bargetto

Castelnuovo d'Asti - *Piazza del Monumento e Via Umberto I.*

Piazza Don Bosco in Castelnuovo.

some of what living in the region might have been like for the Bargetto clan during that era. Born in 1815 in a log cabin, Giovanni Melchior Bosco was raised in a difficult and impoverished environment. His father died when he was just two years old. His early years were spent as a shepherd. His first education came from the parish priest, and later he entered the seminary in nearby Chieri. He moved to Torino, Italy, and established an oratory where young boys could receive basic education and benefit from his generous love, which did not allow for punishment.

Giuseppe Bargetto was born in 1844 to a family of six children. He married Adelaide Conrado circa 1867, and together they had eight children. Filippo was the oldest son, followed by six girls and another son, Giovanni, born in 1885. Giuseppe was a peasant with very little education, perhaps a year or two of school. He owned a pasture with some cattle as well as a small vineyard and winery. At a young age, Giuseppe more than likely would have heard about the Gold Rush in California and, later, that California was an important region for winemaking in the United States. Both of these were two good reasons to answer a powerful calling from California.

In 1890, living conditions in Italy were wretched and deteriorating—socially, politically, economically and agriculturally. There was a global economic depression. But perhaps most directly affecting Giuseppe's life was the weather in Piemonte. Northern Italy is known for its extreme climate, especially in the spring and summer, and the 1880s were particularly harsh for the farmers who depended on good weather for wheat to make pasta, and grapes for wine.

According to church documents, Angelo Carpignano, who was from the Asti area, married Giovanni Bargetto's first cousin, Maddalena Conrado. They were both interviewed in 1986 by John Bargetto. Nearly a century later, this period of bad weather would still be remembered by Angelo and

Maddalena, a story passed down to them from their elders. "Thirteen years of hail in the spring and summer wiped out the wheat, corn and grapes," Angelo would recall. These were indeed tough times for farmers in Piemonte.

By 1890, trans-Atlantic trips on steamships had become significantly reduced in price, owing to the numerous emigrants leaving northern Europe and the sharp competition of the shipping lines. In fact, some were able to make the trip for as little as $10 or $15.

With very little money and without the ability to speak English, Giuseppe Bargetto, 46, and his eldest son Filippo, 15, sailed for New York City. They brought with them their only real personal assets—their integrity, their strong agricultural work ethic and their generations-honed skills in winemaking.

Giuseppe Bargetto's corkscrew.

Bargetto Giovanni Maria
N. 27/7/1680
|
Bargetto Antonio (Maria)
N. 12/9/1705
|
Bargetto Giuseppe Antonio
N. 18/11/1756
M. 30/4/1827
|
Bargetto Giuseppe Antonio
N. 25/1/1795
M. 2/3/1828
|
Bargetto Giovanni Antonio
N. 4/9/1820
M. 30/9/1881
|
Bargetto Filippo
N. 27/7/1847
M. 19/4/1936

Geneology chart showing Bargetto Family in Castelnuovo Don Bosco since circa 1680.

Historic cooperage tools, winery collection.

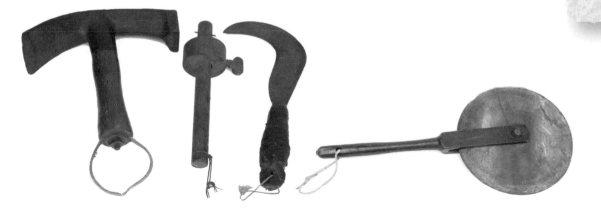

COMPAGNIE GÉNÉRA E TRANSATLA...

The Passenger Act 1882—District of The City of New York, Port of New...

I, G. Collier Master of the St La Normandie do solemnly, sincerely and...

		Age	Sex	Calling	The Country of which Citizen	
140	Hariet do	30	female	none	do	
1	Giuseppe Borretto	46	male	farmer	Italy	
2	Filippo do	12	"	do	do	
3	Jean Moochet	37	"	Shoemaker	French	
4	Marie do	20	female	none	do	
5	Joseph Elwester	25	male	Baker	Switzerland	
6	Barbara do	23	female	none	do	
7	Mélanie Delsol	32	"	Workwoman	French	
8	Léa	14	"	none		
9	Helene	1	"			
150	Theresa Reid	7	b			
1	Louisa	31	male	farmer	Switzerland	
2	Louisa	25	fem	do		
3	Lonia	6	"	none		
4	Frida	2 6	"	"	Germany	
5	Johann Roth	40	male	farmer	do	
6	Ludwig Bieth	28	"	do		
7	Marie do	19	fem	none		
8	Kath Warberger	16	"	maid servant		
150	Anna Schmid	22				

Se ce l'hai fatta tu in America, posso farcela anch'io.
(If you can make it in America, then so can I.)
—*A popular Italian saying from the late 19th century*

Immigration

Chapter Two

Immigration, Original San Francisco Winery
1890-1918

I n the winter of 1890, family patriarch Giuseppe Bargetto and his eldest son, Filippo, left the security of their home town of Castelnuovo d'Asti and set out for the dream known as America—more specifically, California. To board their ship, they first traveled north to the port city of LeHavre, France, where the River Seine flows into the English Channel.

They departed France on February 5, 1890. The trip across the Atlantic took roughly 10 days. Their ocean liner, La Normandie, was a four-masted vessel built in the early1880s for Compagnie Générale Transatlantique (the French Line). She was 459 feet long, powered by steam engines with a single screw propeller, and made a high speed of 17.3 knots—exceptionally fast for her day. While the ship did have limited seating for first-class travelers, the vast majority of passenger accommodations—866 out of 1,109—were in "steerage" as it was commonly known, dedicated to third class passengers. And that is the way that Giuseppe and young Filippo traveled to America.

"They slept in hammocks," according to Maddalena Conrado Carpignano, a first cousin of Filippo. They traveled low in the bowels of the ship in unsanitary conditions. As this was almost certainly their first time being on the high seas, one can only imagine the sea sickness they suffered while in suffocating conditions below deck.

In mid-February they arrived at the Emigrant Landing Depot located at Castle Garden, then operated by the State of New York and located on the southern tip of Manhattan (in Battery Park today), two years prior to the opening of the new federal immigration center on Ellis Island. They were part of epic waves of immigrants from western and then southern Europe during the later half of the 19th century. Once inside of New York Harbor, they were greeted by the Statue of Liberty— Liberty Enlightening the World was its official title—which had been erected on Liberty Island in New York Harbor and dedicated little more than three years earlier.

Giuseppe and Filippo were both formally signed in on the ship manifest of La Normandie. Giuseppe's age was correctly listed at 46 years, and his occupation was shown as "work farmer"—dimin-

Giuseppe Bargetto's home in Italy.

Left: Ship manifest from S.S. Normandie in 1890 showing Giuseppe and Filippo Bargetto.

ishing his role as a landowner and farmer. Filippo's age was mistakenly listed as 12, instead of 15. Perhaps steerage fees were less for those 12 and under, or perhaps it was simply an error in translation or transcription. Whatever the cause of the error, Filippo was actually much closer to manhood than the documentation would indicate.

In 1890, New York City was a hustling, bustling city full of energy—with immigrants pouring in from many nations. The Industrial Revolution was at full throttle. New York was a city at once burdened by grueling poverty, along with unforeseen wealth. That year, the documentary photographer Jacob Riis published a collection of startling imagery entitled *How the Other Half Lives*—a chronicle of ghetto conditions in immigrant

S.S. Normandie on which Giuseppe and Filippo sailed in 1890. Image courtesy Geoffrey Dunn collection.

Left: Mulberry Street, "Little Italy," New York City, circa 1890.
Image courtesy Geoffrey Dunn collection.

Winemaking in Northern California circa 1880 showing Chinese workers. Photo courtesy Geoffrey Dunn collection.

neighborhoods that would resonate nationally and which led the Protestant clergyman Josiah Strong to proclaim that "a mighty emergency is upon us." By mid-decade there would be calls from across the country to establish immigration quotas, particularly for those arrivals from Southern Europe.

The two Bargettos wanted none of the madness of Manhattan or the neighboring New York City boroughs. Shortly after passing through customs and gathering their belongings from steerage, they made their way to Grand Central Station—then, as today, the largest train station in the world—and began their journey across the continent on the Union Pacific and Central Pacific lines, via Chicago. Once on the West Coast, they traveled on the Southern Pacific to their ultimate destination, San Jose, California. It was located in what was a great agricultural center, the Santa Clara Valley, known then as "The Valley of the Heart's Delight."

Father and son, weary from their journey, arrived in San Jose during the dead of winter and soon found their way to nearby Mountain View, where they began work at their ultimate destination, Casa Delmas Winery.

At the time of the Bargettos' arrival, there were three main centers for winemaking in California—Napa Valley, Sonoma and the Santa Cruz Mountains. The Santa Cruz Mountains region then included both the fertile Santa Clara Valley and the steep mountain range that bordered the valley on the west, where many vineyards had been planted beginning as early as the 1850s.

The wine history of the Santa Cruz Mountains is full of periods of boom and bust, and stories of those individuals who pioneered the wine industry in this agricultural center abound. Men like Emil Meyer, John and George Jarvis, and later Paul Masson and Martin Ray—who, although they shared little in terms of national origin, all had a common vision to produce truly great wines. One need only look at the history of winemaking in these mountains—stretching back more than two centuries—to see just how long the region has been associated with unique and outstanding wine production.

The beginning of the Santa Cruz Mountains story can be traced back to the missionary period of the 18th century when Catholic priests, under the leadership of Fr. Junipero Serra and, later, Fr. Fermin Lasuén, directed the first planting of vineyards as part of the early mission communities. These Franciscans brought with them the first European grape cuttings, mostly "mission variety" and Angelica, to Northern California. Although not a yielder of premium table wine, these early varietals greatly influenced the wine of the region until the shift in new plantings during the latter part of the19th century.

The 1880s marked a period of tremendous viticulture expansion in the Santa Cruz Mountains. The entire country was not only growing through waves of immigrants who were accustomed to enjoying fine wines as part of their daily diet, but other Americans were also beginning to enjoy wine consumption on a daily basis.

While Italians, French, German and Portuguese immigrants imported traditions of winemaking to the New World, immigrant Chinese farm laborers and truck farmers played a significant role in helping

Silver dollar from the era of the Bargettos arrival in U.S.

The original crusher de-stemmer driven by a horse and mule at Montebello, circa 1895.

Photo courtesy Ridge Vineyards.

VINTAGE BARGETTO: Celebrating a Century of California Winemaking.

Top: San Jose Train Station, 1890

Middle: Delmas Winery, circa 1895

Bottom: The Santa Cruz Mountain Winery, circa 1890s

to develop viticulture in Northern California. Not only were they among the most efficient workers when it came to harvesting, as historian Richard Steven Street has noted, they also served in a variety of other capacities in the wine industry. This was especially true in the Santa Clara Valley and Santa Cruz Mountains, where Chinese immigrants played significant roles in the development of irrigation and transportation infrastructure (particularly railroad and road construction) and the general expansion of agricultural production. During the 1880s, for instance, the Chinese represented 70 percent of agricultural workers in the Santa Clara Valley.

The years of 1880-1887 saw a fivefold increase in vineyard plantings in the Santa Cruz Mountains region, and by 1891, the counties of San Mateo, Santa Clara and Santa Cruz amazingly had nearly 14,000 acres of planted vineyards. Although not all of these vineyards would lie in what today is the Santa Cruz Mountains region, it was quite typical that the grapes grown in the upper hills would command a higher price than those grown in the valley—owing to the long-established understanding that superior quality grapes were grown in the mountains.

The excellence of these wines was no secret. 1n 1879, Arpad Haraszthy—son of the visionary, albeit reckless, Hungarian born vintner, Agoston Haraszthy—in his statement as head of the California State Viticulture Commission claimed, "as of this date, Santa Clara and Santa Cruz counties can show wines which have no superiors in California."

It was during the 1880s that many of the classic premium European varietals were introduced to the region including Cabernet Sauvignon, Merlot and Zinfandel. Less common cultivars such as Charbono and Chauche-Gris were also planted.

Early Santa Cruz Mountains winemakers were able to understand the potential of these classic grapes. From these initial plantings, the wines produced in the region were receiving rave reviews and winning medals from around the world. In 1889, for instance, the Ben Lomond Wine Company took Honorable Mention at the Paris Exposition for their 1886 Riesling, bottled as a "California White Wine."

It should also be noted that the Santa Cruz Mountains remained relatively wild and untamed during the final decades of the 19th century. The last grizzly bear in the Santa Cruz Mountains was reportedly killed in 1887. Indeed, one of the great characters of the region, Charles Henry McKiernan, known to

Photos and image courtesy Geoffrey Dunn collection.

posterity simply as "Mountain Charley," lost a portion of his skull in a famed battle with a grizzly in 1854. An enterprising doctor famously repaired his wound with a plate pounded out of two Mexican silver dollars. What is less well known about McKiernan is that he later grew grapes in a vineyard near Wrights Station, sold spirits for the Jarvis Wine and Brandy Company, and served as president of the Santa Clara Valley Cooperative Wine Company.

W ine experts from around the world began to note the rich potential of the burgeoning wine industry in the Santa Cruz Mountains area. Charles Bundschu, in his viticultural commission report of 1890, claimed: "The Santa Cruz Mountains district has a good opportunity to show its superiority in many respects. The wines are not very heavy in alcohol, but develop a most delicate flavor and highly distinctive aroma which may be attributable to the proximity of the ocean." In time, the significance of "cool climate" winegrowing would be recognized as a significant factor in the production of fine table wines.

One of the substantial vineyards of the day was Emmett Rixford's La Questa Cabernet Sauvignon vineyard in Woodside. His Cabernet Sauvignon in 1915 won a gold medal at the Panama Pacific International Exposition. The original vine source of this Cabernet Sauvignon is believed to be Chateau Margaux in Bordeaux. His cuttings would later be used for Martin Ray's outstanding Cabernet vineyard overlooking Saratoga, which itself would produce superior Cabernet Sauvignons in the 1940s and 1950s. (The linkage continues to this day, as Bargetto Winery receives most of the grapes from this vineyard.)

In the 1890s, a Frenchman named Paul Masson from Burgundy, France, set out to produce America's finest méthode champenoise, also known as sparkling wine. By mid decade he had purchased property in the Santa Cruz Mountains, to which he gave the name Mount Eden. There he produced Oeil De Perdix (Partridge Eye) the single most successful "Champagne" of the day. His nationally renowned product bore the Santa Cruz Mountains appellation on the label. During Prohibition, Masson produced his sparkling wines with a federal wine permit for "medicinal purposes."

To the south, in Santa Cruz County, in 1883, Dr. John Stewart established the Etta Hill Vineyard in

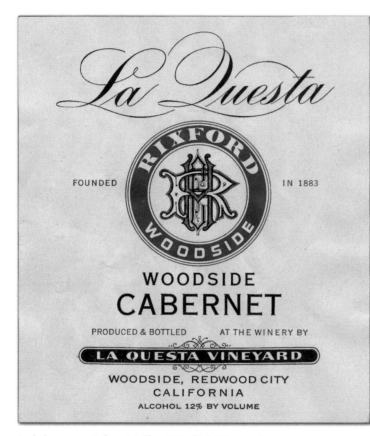

Label courtesy Robert Mullen, Woodside Vineyards.

Scotts Valley, facing Monterey Bay and the Pacific Ocean. There he planted Cabernet Sauvignon, Merlot and Cabernet Franc to blend in the Bordeaux tradition. He sought to produce a fine Sauterne style dessert wine and planted Sauvignon Blanc, Semillon and Muscadelle du Bordellaise. He was the first in the county to utilize resistant rootstock. Later, because of this innovation, his vineyards withstood the ravages of the phylloxera epidemic that wiped out so many of the California vineyards.

So, it was to this booming wine region in 1890 that Giuseppe and Filippo arrived in the Santa Clara Valley, sprawled out in the shadows of the Santa Cruz Mountains. Immediately, they both went to work for Casa Delmas Winery in Mountain View, where each presented a "letter of introduction" on their behalf.

The Delmas family's roots in California winemaking stretched back to the immediate aftermath of the Gold Rush. In 1852, shortly after he first established a nursery in San Jose between the banks of the Guadalupe River and Los Gatos Creek, Antoine Delmas imported the first French grapevines to the state. According to Charles Sullivan, the dean of California wine historians and author of *Like Modern Edens* and *A Companion to California Wine*, Delmas dominated California winemaking awards throughout the 1850s. By 1858 he reportedly owned vineyards with 350,000 vines of 105 varieties. Sullivan contends that Delmas was also a pioneer in advocating the use of elemental sulfur to fight powdery mildew—though he became rather notorious in the 1860s for introducing the ubiquitous California brown snail to the region in an effort to raise escargot.

In the mid-1880s, Antoine's son, Delphin Delmas, a prominent San Francisco Bay Area attorney, purchased a 500-acre ranch near Mountain View to add to the family's ever-expanding agricultural interests. Casa Delmas, as it was known, became one of the largest independent wine producers in the country.

Born in 1844, Delphin attended Santa Clara College and, at the age of 21, received his law degree from Yale University. Only two years later he was elected District Attorney of Santa Clara County. He would later earn national notoriety when he served as the colorful defense attorney for Henry K. Thaw, on trial for killing Stanford White, in what was then dubbed "The Trial of the Century."

By 1887, Delphin had moved to the property in Mountain View (he took the train each day to his law offices in San Francisco) and oversaw the expansion of the winery to a 500,000-gallon operation. When he first incorporated Casa Delmas in 1896, it was valued at $1 million—which today would be worth roughly $40 million. It was an incredibly vast enterprise.

Casa Delmas was the subject of one of the first journalistic accounts by the famous California writer, Frank Norris, whose novels *McTeague* (1899) and *The Octopus* (1901) brought him international literary acclaim. In a lengthy article about a visit to Casa Delmas that he wrote for the weekly California magazine *The Wave*, Norris, in poetic fashion, expressed his surprise of what he found and his "shock to one's perceived notions as to what winemaking should be like." He describes the general condition of California vineyards with distain, "The vineyard itself is disappointing—miles and miles of low green bushes growing out of a hard, flat, dusty soil." At Casa Delmas he continues:

It was at Casa Delmas...and each wagon was weighed in very carefully before it was unloaded... Inside the air was full of the noise of machinery, the coughing of pumps, the clattering of pistons... But what an odour! The odour of torn mashed pulp, the odour of thick, sweet juice—rivers of it, pools, lakes of it ...the welter of a whole harvest; the heart's blood of 500 acres concentrated.

It was in this juggernaut of viticultural activity that the roots of Bargetto winemaking in the region were first established. We know little of either Giuseppe's or Filippo's early activities at Casa Delmas—given their experience, they likely served as wine blenders, fermentation masters and assistant winemakers—but by 1892, after just two years in California, Giuseppe returned to Italy.

According to family history, Giuseppe's return to Italy resulted from the fact that his wife, Adelaide Conrado Bargetto, did not want to leave Italy and emigrate to California. In those days, traditional Italian culture essentially demanded that women did what their husbands asked, so Adelaide's refusal indicates a strong level of independent mindedness on her part and unyielding resiliency. There were seven children remaining in Castelnuovo d'Asti, including 7-year-old Giovanni Bargetto, so perhaps the thought of such a vast uprooting was simply too much to embrace.

When Giuseppe returned to Castelnuovo d'Asti in 1892, he was treated as a hero of the town. A

Left to right: Joseph, Antoine and Delphin Delmas
Photo courtesy Geoffrey Dunn collection.

Giuseppe and his wife Adelaide, seated, with John Bargetto standing at upper left, circa 1905.

parade was given in his honor. After all, he was the first from his village to travel to California and then return again to tell the rich stories of America.

Filippo, 17 years old when his father returned to Italy, continued to work at Casa Delmas. He was now a young man. A decade later, in 1902, records show that he became a U.S. citizen in Santa Clara County. Two years later, Filippo returned to his hometown in Italy and married Francesca Giuseppina Giuliana Turco. Shortly after their return to the U.S. in 1905, Filippo and Francesca moved to San Francisco. They lived on Chestnut Street, in the Portolá District of the city, another center of southern European immigrants. Filippo went to work for a small, local winery. Their first daughter, Sylvia, was born in San Francisco in 1905.

The growing Bargetto family had a fortunate sense of timing. Just two months prior to the Great San Francisco Earthquake and Fire on April 18, 1906, Filippo moved his family back to the security of Casa Delmas and a regular paycheck in Mountain View. A second daughter, Adeline, was born there in 1907. The earthquake and fire devastated much of San Francisco and wrought damage to several other communities in the greater Bay Area, but the Bargetto family avoided the devastation, having relocated down the San Francisco Peninsula.

Right: Procession led by Fr. Giocomo Turco (brother of Ernestina Turco Bargetto), far right, in Castelnuovo Don Bosco.

28

Filippo and Francesca Bargetto
on their wedding day, 1904.
Photo courtesy Bargetto archives.

San Francisco after the Great Earthquake and Fire of 1906. Photo courtesy Geoffrey Dunn collection.

Filippo continued to toil at Casa Delmas and to save his money, but change was coming to the winery. The Trial of the Century took the attention of Delphin Delmas away from the Santa Clara Valley and he would later move to Los Angeles. His son Paul, who was overseeing the winery's operation, unexpectedly lost his 26-year-old wife to a sudden illness in the spring of 1907. His heart was no longer in the business and he would later join his father in Los Angeles.

So it was, in 1909, after nearly two decades of labor at Casa Delmas, that Filippo opened up the first Bargetto family winery in the New World, located at 150 Montgomery Avenue, on the southern edge of San Francisco's "Little Italy," and just above the city's famous Montgomery Block.

That same year Filippo paid for his uncle Giovanni Bargetto (known in the Piedmontese dialect as "Barba Giovanin"), the brother of his father Giuseppe, to join him in California. The two Bargettos and a third partner, Alberto Colombo, formed the South Montebello Vineyard and Wine Company. The Bargettos were involved as principals in other wineries as well, including the Columbus Winery.

Filippo, the most experienced winemaker of the trio, was responsible for the winery's cellar; his uncle John assumed responsibility for the sales floor; while Colombo, listed in the voter registry as a "teamster," handled deliveries to local restaurants and merchants. Grapes were shipped via rail to their San Francisco winery from the Santa Clara Valley, using a network that Filippo had no doubt developed during his two-decade long stint at Casa Delmas. Their wine was fermented, aged and delivered in barrels to local restaurants. In addition, they sold branded wine in bottles under the label South Montebello.

The name of the winery—South Montebello Vineyard and Wine Company—is significant, as it provided a link to the famous vineyard in the Santa Cruz Mountains known as Montebello. In the 1880s, Italian immigrants Vincenzo and Secondo Picchetti were among the first pioneers to plant a vineyard above Cupertino. They named that area of the Santa Cruz Mountains, Montebello (Beautiful Mountain). In 1886, Dr. Osea Perrone, a San Francisco physician, founded a vineyard in the same area and developed a substantial winery, which he specifically named Montebello.

It's likely that the Bargettos, working at nearby Casa Delmas, had some relationship with the vintners in this region. (In 1959, a group led by David Bennion and Paul Draper purchased the winery

Winemaking in the Santa Cruz Mountains, circa 1900.

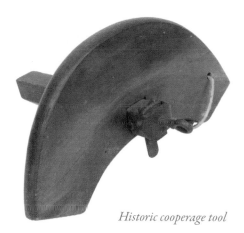

Historic cooperage tool

Bargetto family's first winery in San Francisco called South Montebello Vineyard and Wine Company.
Left photo: Second from left, Filippo, and third from left Barba Giovanin Bargetto.

Below: San Franciscans buying Bargetto wine before Prohibition.

and named it Ridge Vineyards. Ridge's top flight wine would in time come to be known simply as "Montebello," one of the finest Cabernet Sauvignon blends in the country—and completing the circle begun a century earlier.)

What is certain, is that the founding of the South Montebello Vineyard and Wine Company had a significant impact on the history of Bargetto winemaking in the New World. In the fall of 1909, knowing that his uncle and older brother had opened a wine business in San Francisco, 24-year-old Giovanni Bargetto decided to join his family in America. Filippo sent money back home to Italy to help pay for his younger brother's passage across the Atlantic.

Just as his brother and uncle had before him nearly three decades earlier, the younger

Giovanni sailed from LeHavre to the United States. He, too, landed in New York City—in his case, Ellis Island—and made his way west to California's Pacific shores. What precipitated his emigration is undocumented. According to one family story, however, young Giovanni—who had served his country in the Alpini, the elite mountain warfare brigade of the Italian Army—had come home late one night after drinking too much wine, and his father struck him in a heated argument. No doubt Giovanni also would have listened intently to Filippo's California stories five years earlier, when he returned to marry his bride Francesca. Whatever the complex motivations are that led one to leave one's homeland, Giovanni was soon on his way to America.

Dr. Osea Perrone, Monte Bello's founder, circa 1890.

Photo courtesy Ridge Vineyards

The young and single Giovanni joined Filippo and his family in the North Beach neighborhood of San Francisco. Rather than go to work with his brother and uncle, however, he took a job as a dishwasher at the legendary restaurant the Fly Trap. The restaurant was located in the "Barbary Coast," a notorious quarter of San Francisco known for its bars and brothels. Eventually promoted to fry cook, the hard-working Giovanni reportedly labored from sunup to sundown.

Working seven days a week, Giovanni was pushed to exhaustion. A doctor prescribed him relaxation in "the country air." Two years after his arrival in the New World, he moved south, to the ocean side of the Santa Cruz Mountains.

Two of the Bargetto sisters—Angelina and Maddalena—had also immigrated to America, and both married Italian immigrants, Avale Francesconi and Dante Carmignani, respectively. They were part of an expanding Italian community in the Soquel Valley composed of lumberjacks, truck farmers and vegetable peddlers; almost all of them were from Piemonte. In the 1910 United States Census, the sisters and their husbands are listed as living together in Soquel.

In approximately 1911, Giovanni joined his two sisters and their husbands in Soquel. Meanwhile, his older brother Filippo and his uncle, "Barba Giovanin," continued to operate the South Montebello Vineyard and Wine Company in San Francisco. It had earned them a solid living.

During what had been a general era of prosperity for the Bargettos in America, the Bargetto family in the Old World was struggling. Upon his return to Italy, Giuseppe had taken out a loan on a vineyard

The staff at the Fly Trap 1911. Photo courtesy Zare Fly Trap Restaurant, San Francisco, California.

Giovanni Bargetto (19 years old) in Alpini uniform, 1904.

and small winery and could no longer make payments. Brothers Filippo and Giovanni agreed to pay off the loan with the money they had earned in America, and on July 3, 1912, the land and winery were deeded over to them.

Two years later, in 1914, Giuseppe died at 70 years of age. His widow, Adelaide, wrote to her two sons living in California, asking one of them to return to help her with the winery and vineyard. Both sons had staked their claim in America. They never returned to Italy, except to visit.

In the background of the family's entrepreneurial success, however, the drum of the Temperance Movement was beginning to sound. Prohibition was just around the corner. As a result, in 1918 the Bargettos closed down the winery in San Francisco and moved to Santa Cruz for a short time, before joining their other family members in Soquel. (Sylvia Bargetto would later claim that she was told that the family had been swindled by their partner.) By 1919 the Bargettos were all living in sunny Soquel. Yet the darkness of Prohibition had arrived and the family would have to face the latest challenge.

Original Bargetto property known as "L'autin" (Piedmontese meaning knoll); this is the historic site of the Bargetto vineyard and winery in Castelnuovo Don Bosco, Italy.

Old solid brass vat valve.

Ellis Island, circa 1910.
Courtesy Geoffrey Dunn collection.

Once, during Prohibition, I was forced to live for days on nothing but food and water.
—W. C. Fields

Chapter Three

Prohibition
1919-1933

Angelina Bargetto Francesconi, sister to Philip and John, was the first Bargetto to move to Soquel, circa 1910.

Ith the passage of the 18th Amendment in 1919, the Volstead Act—which was enacted by Congress to carry out the amendment's prohibitionist mandate—became the law of the land. It became illegal to possess "intoxicating beverages," and to "manufacture, sell, barter, transport, import, export, deliver, or furnish any intoxicating liquor" anywhere in the United States. One exception to Volstead (named after the Republican congressman from Minnesota, Andrew Volstead, who authored the legislation) was the production of "altar wine," which could still be produced and sold to churches for "religious rituals."

The Catholic Church was a large wine customer, and some California wineries stayed in business during the ensuing 14 years by producing altar wine. (Given the large flow of "altar wine" in the country, some people joked that there were a record number of Catholic masses being conducted on a daily basis.)

Paul Masson, with his vineyard and winery above Cupertino in the Santa Cruz Mountains, was one winemaker who thrived during Prohibition. Ironically, he received a federal license to sell "medicinal champagne."

Decades earlier, Masson planted his vineyard with a special clone of Chardonnay from the world famous Corton-Charlemagne in Burgundy, France. Today, this clone is identified as "Masson" by the Viticulture Department at the University of California, Davis and

Paul Masson had a federal license for "Medicinal Champagne" during Prohibition.

Paul Masson "Champagne" from 1931 Bottle from Charles Sullivan collection.

Left: Federal agents confiscating "bootleg" alcohol.
Photo courtesy Geoffrey Dunn collection.

*The 52-acre Bargetto Ranch,
purchased in 1922, was located in
the Soquel hills and was part of
the original Soquel Rancho.*

is locally known as "Mount Eden" Chardonnay. (Nearly a century after Masson's planting, this same clone was planted at the Bargetto estate vineyard in Corralitos, and in 2013 will yield an anniversary sparking wine.)

With the realities wrought by Prohibition looming on the horizon, the Bargettos closed down their San Francisco winery. The two brothers, Filippo and Giovanni, were now going by the anglicized names of Philip and John, respectively. Philip and his wife Francesca, along with their two daughters, Sylvia and Adeline, moved initially to Water Street near downtown Santa Cruz. A short time later, Philip joined younger brother John, who had been living in Soquel since about 1911 with two of his married sisters, Angelina Francesconi and Maddalena Carmignani, along Soquel Creek (adjacent to the present-day Bargetto Winery). John had purchased a wagon route of vegetable peddling from Gabriel Ciucci, another early Italian immigrant to Soquel.

The 1900 United States Census reveals that it was Enrico Francesconi, an elder brother of the Bargettos' brother-in-law, Avale Francesconi, who first arrived in Soquel as a worker in the lumberyards in what was then known as "Grover's Gulch," in the Bates Creek watershed (today known as Glen Haven). By 1919, Philip and his wife, Francesca, his two daughters, Sylvia and Adeline, along with younger brother John, were all living in the old house on the Brown family land along Soquel Creek, on what would eventually become the Bargetto Winery.

Together, Philip and John expanded their vegetable peddling routes via horse and wagon to the far reaches of the county. They

The iconic Congregational Church was built in 1870. Photo courtesy Capitola Museum.

The Ugo Giomi Hotel in Boulder Creek where Philip and John spent nights while operating their truck farm.

View of the Soquel Valley, circa 1910. Photo courtesy Covello and Covello Photography.

The original home with water tower where the two Bargetto families started residing in 1918.

Soquel was famous for cherries in the 1920s, Geoffrey Dunn collection.

would rise at 3 A.M., feed the horses, and then get an early start for the long trip up the San Lorenzo Valley. Once in the valley, the Italian immigrant brothers were surprised to experience some of the remnants of the wild west before their very eyes. In the 1920s, men still carried pistols in holsters, and occasionally took law enforcement into their own hands.

By 1920—between their work in San Francisco and Soquel—the brothers had saved enough money and purchased the Eugene and Lucy Brown property for $3,000. The full price was $3,300, but Mr. Brown insisted that the remaining $300 go to Sylvia and Adeline. (Years later, and without rancor, Sylvia said they never received the money; everything went back into the Bargetto family pot.) The property came with four acres of land, a house with a basement and an old dirt-floor barn. For the first time since coming to America, the Bargettos were landowners.

By the time the family purchased the property, John was 35 years old and still single. According to family lore, American women were not to his liking, and he thought them to be "a little bit crazy." As a result, he returned to his home town in Italy with his sister-in-law, Francesca. In 1921, he married the youngest sister of Francesca—Ernestina Turco—and brought her back to Soquel.

It is interesting to note that not only did the two brothers marry two sisters, but also one of the Bargetto sisters in Italy, Sandrina Bargetto married Angelo Turco; talk about a tight-knit Italian famiglia—three siblings from one family marrying three siblings from another. (Brothers and sisters marrying into the same family was not an uncommon occurance in Italy during that era.)

Within a few years, the hard-working immigrants were already looking to expand their agricultural enterprise. John Bargetto would often recite his favorite expression: *"Non volgio nascere e morire nel un bicchiere d'aqua"* ("I don't want to be born and die in a glass of water").

A few years later, in 1922, they purchased a 52-acre piece of property in the hills of Soquel above Grover's Gulch, where there was still a familiar community of Italian immigrants. There was also a small general store and elementary school. On the neighboring property, the Bargettos planted plums and cherry trees—as Soquel was famous for cherries in those days. A circular grove of redwoods was used as a natural packing shed for the fruit. In addition they established a small vineyard.

The Bargetto family referred to this beautiful piece of paradise which overlooked Monterey Bay as simply "the ranch." Vittorio Zoppi was another immigrant with long ties to the community of Italian laborers living in Grover's Gulch. He worked on the Bargetto property for decades. He plowed the soil with a mule, pruned the trees and vines and he was known to enjoy a few "sips" of wine during the day.

The decade of the 1920s was a time of expansion, not only in land, but also for the family. The year after Ernestina arrived on the property, she gave birth to the first male of the next generation. In 1922, Lorenzo Silvio Giuseppi Bargetto (later changed to Lawrence Joseph), known as Larry, was born at home on the new Bargetto-owned property. Two years later, in 1924, Raffaelle Vittorio Alberto Bargetto (later known as Ralph) was born.

The vegetable peddling sustained the family financially during Prohibition, but wine remained the Bargetto family's passion. Wine was what they knew best. To Italian immigrants, "vino" was a basic staple of food for the family.

Prohibition laws did permit Americans to produce 200 gallons of wine per year, per household. In the early years, the Bargetto brothers started with that amount, with grapes from the "ranch" which they used for their own consumption. Of course, during Prohibition there was demand for wine.

Many of the locals were selling "rot-gut" wine for profit. Although the Bargettos were upstanding citizens, the concept of Prohibition was hard to grasp. For these winemakers not being able to sell wine was like telling a baker he could not make bread. Furthermore, to add to the family challenges, the cherry trees on the ranch died of some unknown disease.

In 1924, the two Bargetto brothers decided to start what was then called a "bootlegging" operation on their properties. Some of the wine was sold in gallon jugs, which went for one dollar per gallon. However, most of the wine sold was incorporated into dinners that were served to the public on the weekends in the old family home on Main Street in Soquel. Flavorful Zinfandel was served with antipasti, polenta and veal. It was a delicate arrangement that attempted to sidestep the law by charging for the dinner, and including the wine as an added bonus.

John Bargetto, circa 1920.

Ernestina and John Bargetto on their wedding day in Italy, 1921.

41

Sylvia and Adeline in dresses made by their mother Francesca, 1921.

In an interview conducted by California wine historian Charles Sullivan in 1992, Sylvia Bargetto recalled, "If people came to drink, they came in the house. If they came to buy wine, my father (Philip) took care of that. My uncle (John) took care of the parking. He would have a flashlight and direct them where to park. It was all without light. If they just wanted wine, they'd stay in the car."

Sylvia explained the arrangement in further detail: "If they came for dinner, it was $2.50 and that gave them a bottle of wine for every four people. That was part of the dinner. And then they would buy anymore bottles that they wanted. It would be another $2.50 per bottle. The men in the family took care of that. They'd go downstairs and get another bottle. It was a fifth, and I'd bring it to the table. These were nice days."

The Bargetto clientele were the leaders of the community: doctors, lawyers, businessmen and judges. These people appreciated food and wine and could afford an authentic, homemade Italian dinner—and a good bottle or two of wine that went along with it.

There was always concern, of course, about getting caught selling wine and the troubling headlines and articles that would appear in the local papers. It was, in fact, during one of these Sunday night dinners that one of the best Prohibition stories took place—one that Ralph Bargetto would regale others in telling many times over the years.

In the middle of a Sunday dinner at the Bargetto house, with the customers enjoying food and wine and perhaps some Italian songs, a loud knock was heard at the door. A sheriff's deputy had arrived with the intent of arresting the Bargettos for "bootlegging." He barged in and made his presence known in a threatening manner. Much to his dismay, he found a local police chief, a fire chief and a local judge having dinner. He made his apologies and, as Ralph liked to note, "left sheepishly."

Italian lace butterfly.

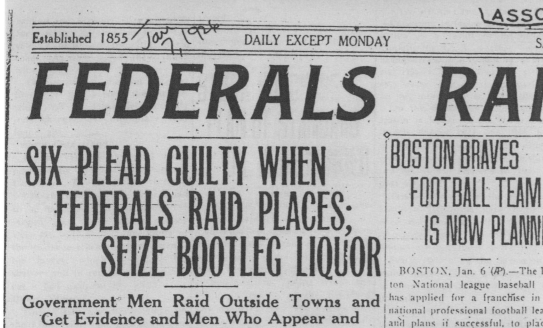

FEDERALS RAI...

SIX PLEAD GUILTY WHEN FEDERALS RAID PLACES; SEIZE BOOTLEG LIQUOR

Government Men Raid Outside Towns and Get Evidence and Men Who Appear and Plead Guilty In Court

Six pleaded guilty to possession of liquor and five were fined $500 each and the sixth, J. Panantoni of the Roma hotel will be sentenced at ten o'clock this morning by Judge C. C. Houck.

Raid by Federals

The raids were conducted under Col. Samuel I. Johnson, assistant to Col. Green of San Francisco. In this raid, 100 per cent successful, he was assisted by 22 federal agents.

They started at Boulder Creek and worked the system known as the zero hour, a new policy followed by Colonel Johnson, the squadron separating and simultaneously entering the places raided at the same time.

The zero hour last night was 9 o'clock.

Boulder Creek Visited

Boulder Creek furnished the raiding squad plenty of excitement for a while. They went to J. Locatelli's place on the Big Basin road. At this place they found wine.

They went to the old Boulder Creek House, across the bridge, where W. D. Alexander, recently took charge. At this place they found gin.

Federal Cuts Hand

...sent a complete substitute program. One after another case was called and tried. Besides Judge Houck, District Attorney Stanford Smith was in court representing the people, and Deputy Sheriff J. A. Beguhl was in court during the entire proceedings and it was nearly one o'clock when the courtroom was cleared.

Each one of the six pleaded guilty and all with the exception of the local man, J. Panatoni, was fined $500. Panatoni will be up for sentence this morning at ten o'clock.

Big Raid

The same group ... biggest hauls in ... valley section on ... They dumped 100 ... mash and seized ... capacity continuous ... At this place seven ... seized.

Following the court ... the entire squad went ... dle Rock for supper.

BOSTON BRAVES FOOTBALL TEAM IS NOW PLANN...

BOSTON, Jan. 6 (AP).—The ... ton National league baseball ... has applied for a franchise in ... national professional football lea... and plans if successful, to plac... selected eleven in the field for ... next two seasons, Secretary Ed ... Riley announced today.

The project was planned par... ularly as an economy addition ... the Braves field baseball p... Riley said, as the leaders of ... National league hope to make ... for many months of baseball i... ness by filling the stands in ... fall and winter months.

The Braves ... league club to ... with professio... though the Ne... season lent thei... to a club...

STOCK PURCHA...
PLAN OF STAN...

CONFISCATED WINE AND LIQUOR DESTROYED BY POLICE DEPT.

The ceremony of destroying all wine seized in late raids was carried out according to a prearranged program this morning shortly before 10 o'clock, when Chief of Police F. Hannah, acting as lord high executioner, and armed with a broad axe, began to knock in the bungholes of eleven barrels of red and white wine, which allowed the contents to seep through a manhole leading to the city sewer ... close to the city prison.

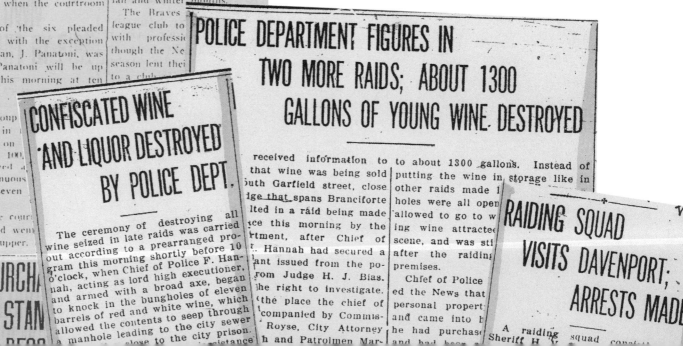

POLICE DEPARTMENT FIGURES IN TWO MORE RAIDS; ABOUT 1300 GALLONS OF YOUNG WINE DESTROYED

received information to ... that wine was being sold ... South Garfield street, close ... ge that spans Branciforte ... lted in a raid being made ... ce this morning by the po... rtment, after Chief of ... Hannah had secured a ... ant issued from the po... rom Judge H. J. Bias. ... he right to investigate. ... the place the chief of ... companied by Commis... Royse, City Attorney ... h and Patrolmen Mar-

to about 1300 gallons. Instead of putting the wine in storage like in other raids made ... holes were all open... allowed to go to w... ing wine attracte... scene, and was sti... after the raiding ... premises.

Chief of Police ... ed the News that ... personal propert... and came into h... he had purchase... and had been ...

RAIDING SQUAD VISITS DAVENPORT; ARRESTS MADE

A raiding ... Sheriff H... squad cons...

Prohibition

"Six pleaded guilty to possession of liquor and five were fined $500...J Panantoni...will be sentenced in the morning by Judge C.C. Houck...

The raids were conducted under Col. Green of San Francisco...In this raid, 100 percent successful, he was assisted by 22 federal agents.

At Soquel:
The last one to be brought to court after the midnight hour was F. Baggetta (sic), who has a place at Soquel, up the creek. The 200 gallons of wine seized here was dumped, and they also found gin."

—January 7, 1926 exerpt from The Santa Cruz Evening News

Bargetto family trip to Italy 1927-28
Front row left to right:
Adeline, Sylvia, Philip, Adelaide,
Lawrence, John, Ralph and Ernestina Bargetto.

November 27, 1927 letter
written at sea by Francesca Bargetto
in Italian to relatives in San Francisco.

With enough money saved from the years of hard work and the rewards of selling their wine, the family decided to travel back to Italy in 1927. This time, fortunately, the Bargettos could afford to travel in style, no longer relegated to the harsh "steerage" conditions of the bilge. They sailed on the Cunard Line, on a ship named Berengaria. Both Philip and John wanted to see their aging mother—and it would turn out to be their final visit. The brothers, their wives and their four children— Sylvia and Adeline, Larry and Ralph— plus nine relatives from Soquel—all went and lived for one full year at the family's home in Italy.

In 1928, the Bargetto clan returned to Soquel after a wonderful sojourn to Italy, but there was tragedy on the horizon. Philip's wife Francesca had been ailing for years, ever since she had been hit by a car while walking to work at the Ciucci Gardens nursery years earlier. (In 1919, a woman driving a Model T Ford did not see Francesca walking on a foggy morning in Soquel and ran over her.) Francesca never fully recovered. She passed away in October, 1928. These were tough times for the close-knit Bargetto family, suffering from the loss of wife, mother, aunt, sister and sister-in-law.

The tragedy spawned resolution. The Bargetto family was an entrepreneurial one, always exploring new business ventures. That same year, they opened a wholesale produce store on Eagle Street in Santa Cruz and later a vegetable and grocery store at 232 Pacific Avenue in Santa Cruz.

Another bolt, however, was about to hit not only the Bargetto family but also the entire nation. In October of 1929, the stock market crashed and sent the American economy into what would eventually become known as the Great Depression. This would hit every sector of American life, including the Bargetto businesses. Years later Sylvia Bargetto would recall how one night the family literally ran out of food, having only a few potatoes to eat.

In 1929, Philip and John, always looking to expand their business, purchased their first truck, a 1929 Ford. John claimed this was the first truck in Santa Cruz County.

By 1932, Lawrence and Ralph were coming of age to work, at ages 10 and 8, respectively. Sylvia and Adeline were by now grown women, although still single. With economic demands weighing hard on the family enterprise, there was hope that the end of Prohibition was in sight.

"Wall Street today passed through the momentous and disastrous period in its colorful existence. The bubble had broken. Millionaires were sent home paupers.

Billions of dollars were lost in the hurricane of tumbling prices. The struggle was titanic."
—The Pittsburg Press

Ralph and Lawrence Bargetto
in Italy, 1928.

Adeline Bargetto showm working in the
grocery and produce store at 232 Pacific
Avenue in Santa Cruz. The store was
called Bargetto Ranch Market and was
operated from 1920 to 1931.

Santa Cruz News, June 18, 1928

Bargetto Brothers Have Big Opening

Santa Cruz housewives have shown their appreciation of Bargetto Brothers Ranch Market, dealing in fresh fruits and vegetables, which opened at 232 Pacific avenue last Friday. Friday and Saturday five clerks were busy taking care of the continual stream of customers from early morning until late at night. During these two days over 2000 sales were made and Saturday by noon stocks of vegetables were so depleted that a call to their ranch for vegetables was necessary. Bargetto Brothers are well known throughout this locality as ranchers. In starting

Francesca and Philip on the Bargetto ranch, circa 1925.

The Grover Gulch Wildcats. Left to right: Jack Malloch (mascot), Harvey Nugent, Clarence Angell, Milton Nugent, Harry Hooper (in white Boston Red Sox hat), Harvey Bradley, Tom Hickey, Jack Bostwick, Eugene Daken, Branch Wallace and Paul Johnston.

Signed baseball. Photo courtesy Geoffrey Dunn collection.

Prohibition...goes beyond the bounds of reason in that it attempts to control man's appetite through legislation, and makes a crime out of things that are not even crimes.
—*Abraham Lincoln*

Chapter Four

Repeal of Prohibition, Soquel Winery Founded
1933-1959

I t took one amendment to the United States Constitution to initiate Prohibition. It would take another to repeal it. On December 5, 1933, with the passage of the 21st Amendment, Prohibition was officially over. (The 19th Amendment gave women the right to vote, and the 20th Amendment changed Inauguration Day from March 6 to January 20.) *"Happy Days Are Here Again,"* as the song went. President Franklin Delano Roosevelt was elected by a landslide in November, 1932, in part because of the Democratic Party's commitment to end Prohibition.

Not coincidentally, it was on December 5, 1933, that Bargetto Winery was formally established. The Bargetto brothers had survived 14 long years of Prohibition, and they were prepared for the new era. The family stayed up all night and bottled and labeled wine so as to have plenty of product for sale on December 5. However, the grip of the Great Depression was now dominating the country, and money was very scarce. To affix the early wine labels to the bottles, Philip and John used flour and water as a simple glue.

"I always laughed that on Repeal Day...we started with vintage wines."
—*Ralph Bargetto (Sullivan interview, 1992)*

The following year, in 1934, Bargetto Winery received its official federal bond and became Bonded Winery No. 3859. Recognizing that they were pioneers of the new emerging California wine world, the Bargetto brothers knew they should support the industry. They became charter members of the California Wine Institute, the leading state-wide trade organization charged with supporting the re-emerging wine industry.

Winemaking in the early years required tremendous physical work. Initially the winery did not even have electricity and the wine had to be pumped by hand pumps. Boxes of grapes were loaded on and off the trucks by hand. The hot fermenting wines needed to be cooled in the middle of the night with

Left: The first Bargetto label used in the 1930s.

Winery founders Philip and John Bargetto.

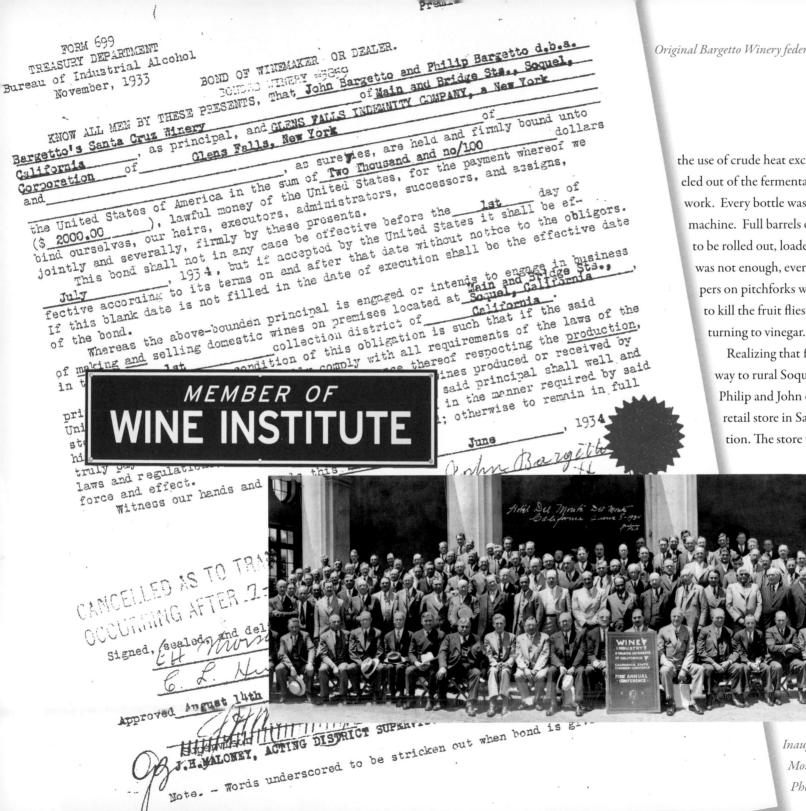

MEMBER OF
WINE INSTITUTE

Original Bargetto Winery federal bond

the use of crude heat exchangers. Grape pomace was shoveled out of the fermentation tanks and was backbreaking work. Every bottle was corked utilizing a hand-corking machine. Full barrels of wine, weighing 600 pounds, had to be rolled out, loaded onto trucks for delivery. If that was not enough, every evening during harvest, newspapers on pitchforks were damped with oil and ignited to kill the fruit flies in the cellars, to avoid the wine turning to vinegar.

Realizing that few customers would travel all the way to rural Soquel to purchase their wine in 1934, Philip and John opened the first wine and liquor retail store in Santa Cruz County after Prohibition. The store was located on Water Street and

Inaugural Wine Institute Meeting,
Monterey, California in 1934.
Photo courtesy California Wine Institute.

Sylvia Bargetto operated the retail store from 1934-1955.

was located just one block from the Santa Cruz Post Office. This historic post office, built in 1912, was inspired by the Foundling Hospital in Florence, Italy. (Filippo Brunelleschi, the famous 15th century architect, designed both the Duomo in Florence and the Foundling Hospital.)

Philip and John viewed the end of Prohibition as a terrific opportunity, but in 1933 the U.S. economy was in the pit of the Depression. Furthermore, at the time, wine was considered a luxury. Once wine became legal, wine prices bottomed out. According to family lore, Grandpa John Bargetto once remarked… "Repeal was the worst thing for the wine business… you couldn't make money anymore."

Sylvia and Adeline worked for years for the good of the family and the business. Whether it was working for the winery directly, or in Adeline's case, at the Ford dealer in Santa Cruz, their earnings always went back to the family. Philip's eldest daughter, Sylvia, operated the Bargetto retail store on Water Street from its opening in 1934 until 1955 when the flooding of the San Lorenzo River in downtown Santa Cruz forced its closure.

The store served as a retail outlet for both wine and hard liquor (including the popular Gordon's Gin). It also was the base for the family's wholesale operation, from which the Bargettos delivered wine in barrels to local restaurants. Unlike today, most novice wine drinkers at the time were unfamiliar with varietal names, so generic names were used in marketing various wines. "Burgundy" suggested a lighter style red wine and "Claret" was used on a richer red wine. People could taste straight from the barrels, and purchase the bulk generic wine for $1.25 per gallon.

Wine was also bottled at this location. In fact, the original bottle with Bargetto Bros. brand shows "Bottled on Water St.," and sold for $.59. This original bottle also demonstrates the long-standing appreciation of mountain-grown grapes, as the bottle features "Select Mountain Vineyard." The Bargettos were way ahead of their time in another fashion. From the start, the finest wines carried the Bargetto brand, and featured varietal wines. This was a time when most consumers hardly knew what wine was, yet, Bargetto sold Zinfandel and Riesling wines. (Charles Sullivan notes that at the time, labeling laws were not strict and Riesling could have included Grey Riesling or even Sylvaner.)

Since moving to the Soquel property in 1918, the two Bargetto families had been living together in the same old ranch house. Sadly, Philip died in April, 1936, just over two years after he realized his

Water Street retail wine store was the first post–Prohibition store in Santa Cruz County.

*John and Ernestine's Italianate home,
built in 1950, is now used for winery offices.*

*Larry in winery laboratory in 1950.
Ralph in WWII uniform, circa 1944.*

*Locatelli's Eagle Rock Vineyard,
Ben Lomond Mountain (now
AVA), in 1948 during a fire that
burned to the ocean
Photo courtesy Harry Locatelli.*

dream of owning a winery in the Santa Cruz area. He had a stroke at the age of 62 and never recovered. His brother John was left to operate both the ranch and the winery himself, with his niece Sylvia operating the Water Street store. John's two sons, Lawrence and Ralph, were just 14 and 12, respectively, and both still in school. As a result, the weight of the family enterprise fell largely on John, who was assisted by a very dedicated worker living on the family property, Vittorio Zoppi.

The small vineyard on the Bargetto ranch was not nearly enough to provide all the grapes for the growing wine operation. The family sought out grapes from area vineyards: Locatelli in Boulder Creek, Beauregard, Quistorff and Iacopetti in Bonny Doon, and Delucchi in Santa Cruz. In addition, the winery received grapes from JSP Cardoza and McGrath in Corralitos. Zinfandel and Carignan were typical red wines produced. The lesser known Beclan was a red wine made from Corralitos grapes. (Beclan is a rare French variety that produces a big, rich wine. There are two sub-varieties, Petite Beclan and Gros Beclan.)

The original winery was little more than an old converted barn, with a dirt floor. A section of that original dirt floor remained in the winery until the 1970s.

John's eldest son Larry graduated from Santa Cruz High School in 1940. He attended Santa Clara University (SCU) in the fall and majored in biology. Later Ralph attended SCU and majored in business. (SCU Professor Fr. Rocatti, S.J., originally from Castelnu-ovo Don Bosco, played a pivitol role in getting scholarships for the boys. The deal came with a promise of home-cooked raviolis by Er-

*Winery cupolas were added to cool
the wine cellars naturally.*

nestina for Fr. Rocatti and SCU President, William Gianera, S.J., both of whom were regular visitors.) Larry was a fine student, particularly in science. He had ambitions to go to medical school and twice applied to Creighton Medical School in Omaha, Nebraska. Both times he was accepted, but decided not to attend, and instead chose to stay with the family business. (His mother, Ernestina, was deeply disappointed by his decision not to become a doctor.) However, Larry's choice to go into the family wine business would prove to be a critical one that would help shape the future of Bargetto Winery in the years to come.

In December of 1941, the United States declared war on Japan, Germany and Italy. Both of John Bargetto's boys were eligible to be drafted, but Larry, in college, received a 4-F deferment because of a heart murmur. Although John was patriotic to his adopted country, he did not want his son Ralph, who had just graduated from high school, to go off to war, especially if it meant fighting in Italy. John even went so far as to set up a pig farm on the ranch and tried to persuade the Army recruiter that Ralph was needed to operate the impromptu farm. The ruse failed. Ralph was drafted and went off to war in Europe.

Ralph served in the 13th Armored "Black Cat" Division in General George S. Patton's Army and rose to the rank of corporal. He participated in both the Rhineland and Central Europe Engagements, including the Battle of the Bulge, and spent at least one night in the snow nearly freezing under an Army tank. He earned two battle stars.

While Ralph was away at war, his father, his cousin Sylvia and brother Larry held down all three operations—the winery, ranch and retail store. With his brother deceased and being cash-strapped, John felt a heavy burden. In 1944, John decided to sell the 52-acre ranch on Glen Haven for $37,000. This translates to a bit more than $700 per acre.

For decades after the sale, the family would bemoan this decision to sell the land. This prime and sunny location above the fog line, with deep alluvial soil, could have provided tremendous opportunities for the family to grow super premium grapes. (It would be nearly 50 years later before the Bargetto family would once again own vineyard land.) Nonetheless, what John decided to do with the proceeds from the sale of the ranch would prove

*Bargetto cousins Norma and Emily
Arpan in the 1929 Ford truck.*

Original magnum of Bargetto wine from 1933.

Original labeled Bargetto wine bottle sold for $.59.
Below: John Bargetto on ranch vineyard at harvest time in 1938.

Redwood wine tanks in cellars used from 1949 until 2006.
Inset left: Adeline Bargetto next to original Bargetto sign.

Ebulliometer, for testing wine alchol.
Below: Historic brass and copper
wine filter used in the 1930s.

Ralph bottling Zinfandel, 1950.
Photo Covello and Covello Photography
Below: Historic hand pump used in 1930s.

Original hydrometers used to
measure sugar level in juice and
alcohol in wine.

Below: Wine "thief" used to
sample barrels.

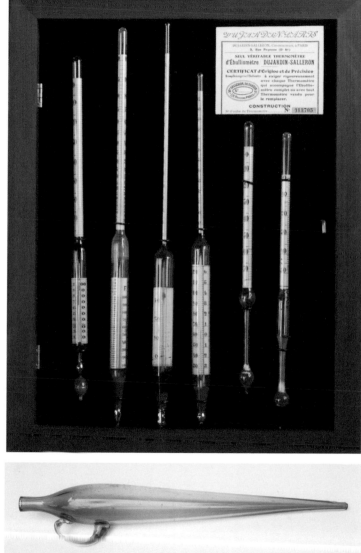

Petri bottling line, circa 1949.

to be significant. He would complete three visionary expansions with the funds.

First, with both sons now graduated from Santa Clara University, John decided in 1949 it was time for a winery expansion and he had the capital in hand from the ranch sale to execute the growth. He completed the largest expansion ever at the winery by adding 8,000 square feet to the operation, more than doubling its size. $12,000 was spent on the new buildings. The cellars were designed and constructed by a prominent Swedish shipbuilder. Premium rough-sawn redwood was used for the construction. Distinctive cupolas were built to allow for natural cooling of the cellars. Two new rooms were added to the original winery building, one for fermentation and one for aging.

A second major use of the ranch funds was to purchase the tanks to fill up the new rooms. In 1949, Petri Winery in San Francisco, one of the largest wine producers in the country, was selling its tanks from its winery operation. For a fire sale price, the Bargettos were able to purchase numerous used wine tanks which were in excellent condition. Just prior to the harvest of 1949, John, Ralph and Larry and two workers went to San Francisco and loaded the tanks onto box cars and railed them to the train depot in Capitola, roughly a mile south of the winery. The tanks ranged in size from 500 gallons to 12,017 gallons. All the tanks were shipped whole, except the largest, which did not fit on the railcar and had to be broken down and re-assembled at the winery.

All of the larger tanks were made out of old-growth, vertical-grain, redwood trees. (Today, this rare wood can

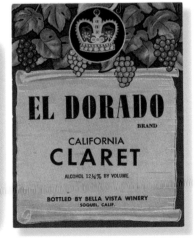

56

be seen in the LA VITA room at the winery.) Ten smaller 100-year-old German oak casks were added as well. These casks ranged between 500 and 1,000 gallons. (Some of these historic casks were used until 2005.) In one ambitious harvest-time purchase, the Bargettos added 72,000 gallons of aging capacity. John's dream was realized and the winery was poised for significant growth.

Finally, that same year, 1949, John and Ernestina started working on a new home of Mediterranean design along Soquel Creek, adjacent to the winery. They used the best supplies in constructing the stucco walls on the exterior, coved plaster walls in the interior, and a red tile roof. A full basement was built with doors wide enough for barrels, and a special pump-drain was included in case Prohibition returned. This new home reminded them of the elegant homes in Italy, of which they had only dreamed. The American Dream seemed to be finally within their reach.

In winter of 1955, heavy rain forced the San Lorenzo River and Soquel Creek over their banks. Flooding damage was serious in both Santa Cruz and Soquel. The Bargettos got hit twice. First, the store on Water Street was flooded and had to be abandoned. In Soquel the raging river entered the back of the winery. Larry would later say how he feared for his father's life as John worked to save some barrels from the torrent. These hardworking farmers knew Mother Nature was not always gentle. The 1955 flood was a serious, although relatively short-term, problem for the Bargettos. However, the greatest threat to the family winemaking tradition lay just around the corner.

John with gold medal winning Zinfandel in 1950.

1955 Flood forced closure of Water Street store and caused serious damage to Soquel.

The third generation of SCM vintners, Larry, Ralph, Micky and Beverly.

*We stand today on the edge of a New Frontier–the frontier of the 1960s–
a frontier of unknown opportunities and perils... the times demand new
invention, innovation, imagination, decision.*
—John F. Kennedy, July 15, 1960

"The Boss" Era

Chapter Five

"The Boss" Era, Modern Winery Emerges
1960-1982

Then the 1950s brought prosperity and rapid economic growth to the United States and much
of the same to Bargetto Winery. Brothers Lawrence and Ralph married college-educated
beautiful brides, and began starting families of their own. Ralph married Marguerite (Micky)
Garnier from Burlingame on April 15, 1950. On June 19, 1954, Lawrence took his wedding vows with
Beverly Regan from San Francisco.

The two brothers, along with their father, John, used the large expansion in 1949 to transform the
winery into a greater thriving enterprise. By now Bargetto Winery was establishing a name for itself
beyond the confines of Santa Cruz County.

If the 1950s were a time of relative national tranquility, the 1960s marked a decade of upheaval with
civil rights unrest and conflict over the Vietnam War. Locally, the University of California Santa Cruz
(UCSC) brought considerable changes to the region and a new and unforeseen infusion of student
protests and activism in the community.

It was a time of significant transition at the winery as well. Wine appreciation in the United States
was still very limited. In fact, wine consumption was dominated by dessert wines like Sherry and Port. It
was not until 1967 that table wine consumption first surpassed dessert wine consumption in this country.

By the 1960s, Larry and Ralph had taken on major responsibilities at the winery for more than a
decade. Their father John had slowed down considerably and he had handed over the reigns of the
operation to his two college-educated sons. With his education and knack for science, Larry focused
on wine production, improving wine quality and building a laboratory for testing the wines. Ralph, the
more outgoing of the two brothers, was a natural salesman and traveled around Santa Cruz, Monterey
and the San Francisco peninsula to sell the various Bargetto products.

By this time, Bargetto Winery had long since stopped selling wine in barrels. Instead, the winery had
established brand sophistication for its bottled wine. The winery had three key brands, each of which
offered wine at a different quality and price tier. The least expensive wine was sold in gallon jugs, under

Bargetto Winery exterior, 1968

Lawrence J. Bargetto (Larry), 1980.
Photo courtesy Jim Hobbs.

59

*Photo of Larry credited to Ansel Adams,
who visited the winery July, 1967.*

the JB brand (for "John Bargetto") for wines like Burgundy. El Dorado brand (Ralph's idea) was also used for gallon-size generic wines.

The next wine tier was Winemaster. (This brand was later sold in the 1970s to Guild Winery for $10,000.) Winemaster brand was used for generic wines like Chianti, Rhine Wine and other mid-priced wines. These wines were sold in gallons, half-gallons and "fifths," so-called because they were a fifth of a gallon. The fifths retailed for just $.79 per bottle. (In 1975, the U.S. wine industry converted to metric measurements and each bottle now held 750 milliliters.)

The finest and most expensive wine carried the Bargetto brand. Under the Bargetto label during this era, varietals such as Zinfandel, Sylvaner and Chardonnay were sold.

By the early 1960s, Larry and Ralph were each living on the original winery property, as their father had given each of his sons a lot on which they built their family homes. By 1964, their families combined now had 13 children. Ralph and his wife Micky had nine (Philip, Thomas, Ann, James, twins Peter and Paul, Mary, Catherine and Teresa). Larry and his wife Beverly had four (Martin, Loretta, John and Richard). The final child for each family, Rita and Donna respectively, arrived in the summer of 1968 to make a total of fifteen children. The property came to be called "the Bargetto Family Compound," with an exceptional amount of youthful vitality.

Financial pressure had been building on the ever-expanding families for years. Cousin Sylvia, at 51 years of age, married Italian immigrant Frank Merlo in 1956. After getting married, Sylvia left the wine business. Wine sales were growing but were not expansive enough to support these two rapidly growing families. In 1963, it was decided that Ralph would leave the business to explore and develop real estate pursuits, and the winery paid for him to earn his real estate license.

Ralph went on to have a very successful career in real estate in Santa Cruz County. He started a realty company called Real Estate Center and opened six offices, initially with three partners. Later he mused that he should have gone into real estate even sooner. Not only was Ralph a successful business man, but he also became an influential civic leader in the region. He went on to become the president of the Dominican Hospital Board, Goodwill Industries, Rotary Club of Santa Cruz and the Santa Cruz Chamber of Commerce. Ralph also joined the boards of the real estate ethics committee and Long Marine Lab.

Both Larry and Ralph had long been involved with St. Joseph's Catholic Church in Capitola. For years, they both volunteered on the finance committee and fraternal organizations, including Knights of Columbus and Italian Catholic Federation.

As a result of Ralph's career transition, the winery stock was transferred in 1963 from John and Ernestina, Sylvia, Adeline, Ralph and Micky, and consolidated with Larry and Beverly. The transition bore tremendous uncertainties along with great responsibilities. With empty wine tanks and large debt a reality, the future of the winery was in profound jeopardy.

In 1964, at the age of 78, John Bargetto passed away after having surgery for a brain tumor. These were dark days for the winery and family. The founder of the winery and patriarch of the family was gone. The winery was struggling financially; sales were slow. The majority of the wine tanks were empty. Wine names were merely written on the tanks to give the impression that there was wine inside. The winery was saddled with heavy debt. In fact, the winery's debt was larger than the value of the winery itself. Everyone in the family advised Larry to sell the winery, before he lost not only the winery but his family home as well. It was a critical time for Larry to make the decision to either walk away from the business or to take a great risk. With support from his wife Beverly, Larry, against all odds, decided to double-down on the family legacy.

Ralph Bargetto (left) operated the Real Estate Center, 1967-1995.

PAVLVS VI PONTIFEX MAXIMVS
AVREVM NOMISMA
CVIQVE CONSTITVTVM SINGVLARITER DE RE CHRISTIANA
BENEMERENTI

Larry was involved with the Ecumenical Movement that followed the Second Vatican Council in Rome 1962-1965. For his work, Larry in 1965 was given the papal BENEMERENTI (latin for "good works") award by Pope Paul VI.

With plenty of work facing him at the winery, Larry proceeded with ambitious plans. Sensing that the country was now ready to purchase premium California wines, and recognizing the distinctive quality of the Santa Cruz Mountains wines, Larry sought to expand the operation. In order for him to realize his vision to produce truly great mountain wines, he realized that he needed a vineyard of his own, and that Bargetto Winery needed a major modern renovation. He had both ambition and vision. The only missing ingredient was capital.

In early 1966, Irving Berlin Kahn of New York City visited Bargetto Winery. He was the nephew of Irving Berlin, the famous musical composer. Kahn was a founder of the cable television giant, Tele-prompter, and later sold the company for millions of dollars. With Kahn's expressed investment interest, Larry developed an ambitious plan to plant a 115-acre vineyard, most likely in southern Santa Cruz County. He prepared a detailed prospectus that laid out costs for the vineyard, including land which was priced at $2,000 per acre at the time. In addition, the plan called for a major modernization of the winery operations, including a new German-made Wilmes press, stainless steel tanks and even "utilities, telephone and telegraph" for $2,500 per year. The capital required for the entire project was $625,000.

Larry augmented his business prospectus with a letter of support from the distinguished UC Davis viticulture professor, Albert Winkler. Winkler had been a lead researcher and developed the idea of matching wine varietals with specific regions in California. He divided California into five regions, from the coolest Region 1 to the warmest Region 5.

In the early 1960s, Larry took winemaking courses at the University of California, Davis, from noted professors like Maynard Amerine. Unfortunately, the deal for the new vineyard and winery never came to fruition, yet Larry never lost his vision of establishing a vineyard in the Santa Cruz Mountains (SCM).

Larry, always the innovator, looked instead for ways to expand the wine sales. Since 1960, the winery had been operating a small tasting room at the winery. (In the late 1950s there was also a Bargetto tasting room in Los Altos.) At the time, a wine tasting room was a very novel idea. The concept of allowing complimentary tasting of wine for customers was not well established. The wine boom of the 1970s was still far off. It would not be until the 1980s that wine tasting rooms in California would really become popular. Larry was ahead of his time.

In 1967, Larry decided to open a second tasting room. Federal law allowed wineries with the older winegrower license to have two tasting rooms, one at the winery and one at an off-site location. Wanting to reach a new group of tourists in the region, Larry decided to open one on Cannery Row in Monterey. In 1967, Cannery Row was not the developed tourist destination place that it is today. (The aquarium did not open until 1985.) Rather, it was a place of dilapidated warehouses and abandoned sardine fisheries. Cannery Row was also famous for mysterious fires burning down the old buildings. Yet, Larry saw the potential of the area. The two mainstay restaurants on the Row were the Sardine Factory and Kalisa's. Although the Row was undeveloped in 1967, it held a historical mystique due to the writings of John Steinbeck's famous novel, *Cannery Row*.

Legendary Viticulture Professor Albert Winkler.
Photo courtesy UC Davis

To make the Soquel tasting room successful, Larry knew he needed someone with personality and enthusiasm. He found all that, and more, in Patricia M. Ballard. Patti was first hired on the bottling line and quickly promoted to the tasting room. From 1969 until 1994, Patti was a fixture at the tasting room in Soquel. She developed a long list of steady customers who would return regularly to taste the latest vintages. She would pour them a range of wines from Pale Dry Sherry to Ruby Cabernet, from Chardonnay to Barbera.

"This area (SC) will produce top premium quality table wines...I would suggest Chardonnay, White Riesling and Gewurztraminer for the white wines and Pinot Noir for the red wine".
—Albert Winkler

With Patti's personal touch, enthusiasm, customer service, and just a few tall stories to add to her unique entertainment quality, sales grew steadily. In 1975 Larry expanded the Soquel tasting room to include a hand-carved bar and creekside view. Later he added the creekside courtyard area for picnics. Soon there would be an outdoor tasting area as well. On the weekends each bar would be "three deep," with live music playing. Retail sales were booming. At the time, Bargetto was the only bonded winery in Santa Cruz with a tasting room, and many wine lovers were congregating there. The hand-truck was busy rolling out cases of wine to customers' cars.

1962 Gold medal for Zinfandel.

During the 1970s, Vine Hill Vineyard (known formerly as Schemerhorn) continued to supply Chardonnay and Sylvaner grapes to Bargetto. Zinfandel and Carignan arrived from Gilroy from vineyards like Tony Bonino's vineyard. Grapes were shipped in 40-pound wooden lugs and were hand dumped into the Garolla crusher.

Bargetto Soquel tasting room, circa 1975.

Right: Bargetto Cannery Row tasting room, circa 1975.

The 1960s were an era of experimentation in many ways. Natural wines and whole foods were becoming popular. Larry decided to innovate with a new wine type: pure fruit wines. The Bargetto property had delicious Santa Rosa plums and the county was well known for berries. In the summer of 1967 he started with plum wine and it won a gold medal at the California State Fair. During the 1970s he would expand the fruit wine line to include olallieberry, raspberry, pear and

A few Earthtone labels from the 1970s.

Promotional advertisement, circa 1970 featuring Bargetto 1964 Burgundy which then sold for the astronomical price of $10 per bottle.

Patti Ballard in cellar with Larry, 1969.

apricot wines. Soon he developed Mead, a honey wine with a long history, one that predates grape wine. In the earliest version, Mead carried the Bargetto brand, but Larry soon shifted the mead to the more literary name of "Chaucer's," making the historic connection with England's medieval book called the *Canterbury Tales* written by Geoffrey Chaucer.

Vine Hill Vineyards
Scotts Valley, Ca. 95066

November 1, 1974

		1970.00
#9850 Pinot Chardonnay Grapes	4.925 tons @ 400.00	2992.00
#14,960 White Riesling Grapes	7.480 tons @ 400.00	1292.00
#12,920 Sylvaner Grapes	6.460 tons @ 200.00	297.00
#2970 Pinot Blanc	1,485 tons @ 200.00	
		$ 6551.00

July, 1974 grape pricing for Vine Hill Vineyards.

Door carved by Terry King of the Flying Barn Brothers of Santa Cruz.

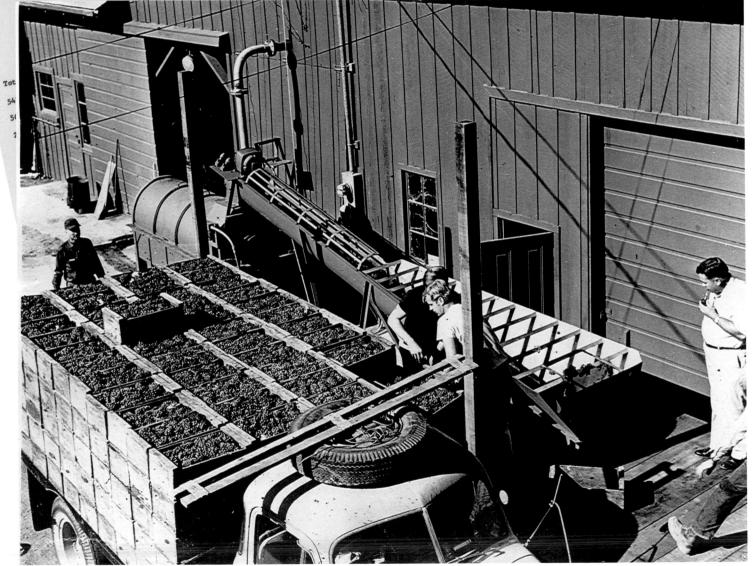

Larry (left) and Bob Hanna (right) watch as grapes arrive in 40-pound lugs, circa 1968.

In the 1970s the fruit wines were a hit. The tasting rooms were thriving as interest in wine soared. Larry and Patti had a wine to offer everyone who parked in the gravel parking lot. The decision to produce fruit wines was a double-edged sword. The fruit wines generated interest and revenue for the winery, and received many gold medals that demonstrated that the wines were considered perhaps the finest in the country. However, in time, there would be confusion in the crowded marketplace about the image of Bargetto. Was Bargetto to be known as a producer of fine SCM varietals, or specialty dessert wines? With a wine for every purse and palate, Larry called his place, "the people's winery."

In 1970, Larry successfully planted three small vineyards in the Soquel area with Pinot Noir vines from David Bruce Winery in Los Gatos. The first was barely one acre on the original Bargetto Winery property. The other two vineyards were planted in the Monterey Bay Heights area of Soquel on the Dr. Gerald Horn property (two acres) and Dr. Charles Devlin land (four acres). Unfortunately, these vineyards were lost to nematodes (soil parasites), divorce and financial problems, respectively.

However, Larry did not give up on his vision to establish a premier Santa Cruz Mountains vineyard. Although the deal with New York businessman Irving B. Kahn in 1966 never materialized, Larry returned to the Corralitos (southern Santa Cruz County) area to hunt for vineyard property. Once again he needed a financial investor. In 1972 he believed that he found one in Dr. Robert Stohler of Pacific Palisades, California. Larry identified a 47-acre apple orchard in Corralitos. The cost per acre was $3,200.

Again, Larry enlisted the services of UC Davis. Viticulture Professor Lloyd Lider gave a positive report on the property. The deal to purchase and plant the vineyard looked to be so certain that Larry

Mead labels from 1963 to present

Stock wine label, Stecher-Traung Printing, San Francisco

Illustration by Arn Ghigliazza

Illustration by Ed Penniman

Illustration by Marilyn Churchill

Illustration by Ed Penniman

Illustrations by Ben Garvie

Ann Bargetto pictured standing fourth from left.

Larry Bargetto (upper right) next to George Barrington with winery employees, 1972.

went ahead and ordered 24,000 vines in anticipation of planting in 1973. (His son John remembers visiting the site as a young boy in winter time.) The numerous varieties to be planted included Riesling, Gewurztraminer and Pinot Noir.

Just prior to the close of escrow, Dr. Stohler and his attorney threw Larry a curve ball. Before proceeding, they insisted on having an equity position in the winery. Larry, in what had to have been a heart-wrenching decision wrote that after a "heart and soul reflection," he did not want to sell any interest in the winery. Close to being complete, the deal fell through. A makeshift nursery was established in the winery front orchard and all the vines were sold to local vineyardists.

Larry continued to pursue his goal to produce the best wine in California. In 1976, Larry purchased the winery's first stainless steel tanks and a refrigeration system to ferment the white wine cool. This was a huge quality improvement. He purchased French

Larry Bargetto's father and uncle were two pioneers of the California wine industry, when the industry was re-starting on the ashes of Prohibition. They provided early support to the wine business by being founding members of the Wine Institute.

Larry was a wonderful man who brought his personal integrity to the winery by the way he operated his winery, and brought an awareness of the high quality of wines in the Santa Cruz Mountains.

—*John De Luca, President, Wine Institute President (1975-2003)*

Larry with record number of gold medals from L.A. County Fair, 1975.

"Limosin" oak barrels and a French-made Vaslin press. In 1976, leading wine writer, Robert Lawrence Balzer of the *Los Angeles Times*, wrote that the 1974 Bargetto Vine Hill Chardonnay was "one of the best in the nation."

Larry continued to innovate with wines. As is the case in many fields of study, some innovations are planned and others arrive from "unanticipated discoveries." In 1978, Larry received Zinfandel grapes from Templeton grower Dan Roy of Farview Farms. The sugars were very high at 27 Brix (grape sugar measurement) and Larry wanted to reject the grapes, yet he proceeded with the production. The wine turned out have to have an alcohol level of 16.1 and had some residual sugar. The timing could not have been better, as this style of late harvest "table" wine was beginning to emerge in the market. The wine garnered a gold medal at the leading competition L.A. County Fair. Larry set the price at $6 per bottle and the wine turned out to be a raging success.

In the 1970s, with growing interest in winemaking, a new breed of UCSC students got their start in the wine business by working in the Bargetto cellars. Under the direction of winemaker Gary Hada, Dawnine Sample, Bill Dyer and Fred Pederson all worked in production. (Dawnine and Bill went on to become winemakers in Napa at Domaine Chandon and Sterling, respectively.) Steve Manildi, Jeff Booth, Nancy Davis, Charlie Devlin and Tim Biancalana also worked in production for Bargetto Winery. Steve, Jeff and Nancy went on to work for Sebastiani, Conn Creek and Mondavi, respectively. Charlie and Tim continued in the wine business as well. Bargetto was indeed a launching pad for budding winemakers.

In 1976 Larry hired UC Davis-trained winemaker, Kevin Tamaki. Kevin led a team of three university enology grads, Janos Radvanyi, Brad Bueller and Dean Sylvester. Janos, Brad and Dean, after cutting their teeth at Bargetto, all went on to have significant

Inaugural wine club news letter, September 1980.

Bargetto

Bargetto Winery
3535 North Main Street
Soquel, California 95073
(408) 475-2258

September 1980 - Release #1

Dear Bargetto Wine Club Member:

Thank you for joining Bargetto's exclusive wine club. As mentioned in the earlier letter you received, this is the first time that we have shipped our preferred customers new wines as they are just released. The response on our initial mailing was tremendous, and all of us at the winery are pleased you joined us in the infancy of our club.

Those of you who have sampled at the winery, or at our tasting room on Cannery Row in Monterey, are already familiar with our wines. Through tasting and talking with our wine counselors, you know we do everything possible to achieve maximum quality in all of our small lots of wine. With our first release, as with the ones to follow, we will explain all the significant steps we took from harvest to bottling. You should have a thorough understanding of that wine after reading this newsletter and while tasting your selection.

Our first Wine Club release is: 1977 Cabernet Sauvignon.

Vineyard Source: Shell Creek Vineyard, Shandon in San Luis Obispo County
Harvest Date: October 13, 1977
Harvest Sugar (°Brix): 26.9
Total Acid at Harvest (g/100ml): .91
Total Acid at Bottling (g/100ml): .54
Residual Sugar (°Brix): Dry
Average Fermentation Temperature: 68°F
Alcohol (%): 13.1%
pH: 3.85
Total Production: 925 cases

To date this Cabernet has had a very rewarding life. On October 13, 1977, 13½ tons of grapes were harvested for this

"Uncle Larry built the success of the winery primarily on the retail rooms. In wanting to assist him to expand retail sales, I tried to think of an innovative way to get Bargetto wines to our devoted customers in a convenient and steady way, beyond their regular visits. Eureka! The Bargetto Wine Club. I never imagined I was creating something that would become so vital to Bargetto and so many California wineries."

—*Jim Bargetto*

careers in the wine industry. Also in 1976, the reputation of California wines internationally soared after the so called "Judgment in Paris" tasting, when California wines bested their French counterparts.

The late 1970s and early 1980s were also a time when late harvest dessert wines became very popular. These wines were produced in the fashion of the great Sauternes of France and Trockenberenauslese of Germany. Larry, again the experimenter, was willing to explore a new style of wines produced from late harvest grapes from Tepusquet Vineyard in Santa Maria Valley, owned by Louis Lucas. This sprawling vineyard was home to 1,750 acres of winegrapes, planted mainly to Chardonnay, Riesling and Gewurztraminer.

In 1980, Ralph's son James (Jim) Bargetto was the national sales manager for Bargetto Winery. Jim wanted to develop a way to increase the frequency of people enjoying Bargetto wines. While in a bar with his college buddy, Jim developed an innovative concept. He outlined the idea on the back of a napkin. Jim envisioned shipping wines on a monthly basis to people's homes. In September of 1980, with Uncle Larry's blessing, Jim launched the "Bargetto Wine Club." At the time, Jim was not aware of any other California winery having a wine club. Bargetto Winery was perfectly poised for this wine marketing innovation, as it produced a full range of wines, and operated two tasting rooms. The tasting rooms were a vital conduit from which new members could join. In time, wine clubs became common in California wineries, and would become the lifeblood of most small wineries.

By the early 1980s, the wine industry was becoming more sophisticated and it was time to establish more specific viticultural areas. Wine-developed European nations such as France and Italy had well established appellations like Bordeaux, Burgundy and Chianti for decades. In 1981, under the leadership of Ken Burnap of Santa Cruz Mountain Vineyard and Dave Bennion of Ridge Vineyards, the Santa Cruz Mountains AVA (American Viticultural Area) was approved by the BATF (Bureau of Alcohol, Tobacco and Firearms—now TTB or Tax and Trade Bureau). Charles Sullivan testified at the hearings on the rich history of the region. This distinct and historical region was the first in the nation to be defined by a

Below: Soquel village was severely damaged by the January, 1982 flood.

Santa Cruz Mountains Appellation map.

mountain range. (At the region's unifying "coming-out wine tasting" in 1991, the motto "America's Premier Mountain Appellation," was introduced and is still used today.)

In January of 1982, a natural disaster hit Santa Cruz County. El Niño storms dumped heavy rains onto the Santa Cruz Mountains, and Soquel Creek (as well as the San Lorenzo River) flooded the town of Soquel. Three feet of water ran through downtown Soquel, causing major damage to the town, but only minor damage to the winery.

In December of 1982, tragedy struck the Bargetto family and winery. While driving back from the Monterey Wine Festival, Larry suffered a stroke. Larry, just 60 years old, died five days later. This was a complete shock to everyone. Larry and Beverly's five children, ages 14 through 25, were not yet involved in the winery; Larry's son Martin has just returned from UC Davis several months earlier. Nephews Thomas (Tom) and Jim Bargetto were working in sales at this time. Without warning, the winery had lost its leader and this tight-knit family had lost a loving husband, father and uncle.

The future of the winery was once again very uncertain.

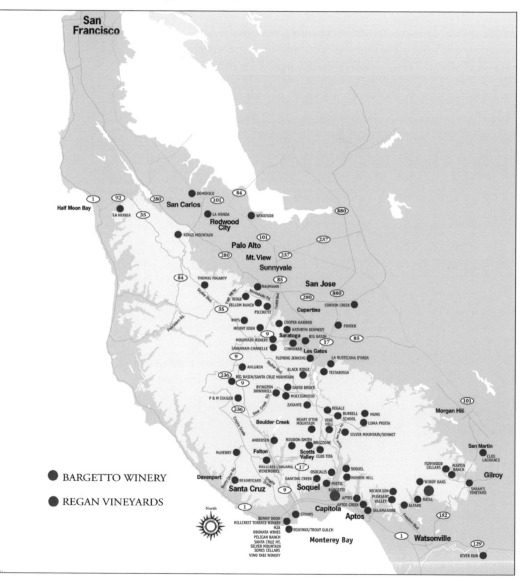

My recollections of "Uncle Larry"
Tom Bargetto

As kids we picked up cigarette butts and dropped them into the Folgers coffee can and tried to leave most of the gravel on the ground. We also washed empty gallons in the long wooden sinks at the back of the winery. Uncle Larry provided us with the work after school and it paid more than doing homework. The winery was also a wonderful place for hide-and-seek, and the creek behind our house was accessible for fishing, swimming, and "temporarily" drowning each other.

"The times they are a changin'..." penned Bob Dylan, in 1964. By now, I was 12 and didn't know much of anything, but I knew that winery work was very physical and I remember lots of the characters that worked with my uncle. Older brother Phil was the first of the nephews to work in the cellars. One of the most interesting and colorful people was a hairy man of biblical proportions. His name was Father John, an Episcopal priest, who worked in the cellars during the week and said mass on Sundays. He enjoyed going into the big redwood tanks and scrubbing the walls clean with a bristly nylon brush and really hot water while singing and taking a steam bath in the "altogether." He would poke his hairy hobbit head out the tank door as a group of tourists would arrive and warmly caution them that he was naked. And of course, that's when the folks would greet Fr. John and all his bristles! Amen. The priest and the uncle would certainly enjoy talking philosophy while a cloud of smoke would rise and hover over their heads from my uncle's omnipresent King Edward brand cigar. It was like incense at high mass.

Our uncle was proud of the family wine tradition. But in most ways he was a very modest man, thoughtful, kind, engaging and truly caring about other people. He was a highly intelligent and sensitive man who would never think that one person was better than another. He was able to talk to a university president, U.S. congressman or the seemingly lowliest person. In his eyes, everybody had worth, and everybody had a story to tell. His Christian faith and the entire family were the most important things to him. I thought the world of Uncle Larry, and I popped into the house often just to chat, borrow the '55 Bel Air, or use his moral compass. He was really a theologian who happened to own a winery.

Grandma's house was near the middle of the property and during the summer I would often meet Uncle Larry there for a fabulous Piemontese lunch. Grandma taught me my first full sentence in Italian and Uncle Larry wisely unveiled the lessons of life. This is where my life-long relationship started with my uncle. Both had wine for lunch and afterward I got a demi-tasse of Medaglia D'oro coffee and biscotti while grandma rested and prayed for all the people written down in her spiral notebook.

Tom Bargetto sampling wine with "the Boss," 1979.

Photo courtesy Jim Hobbs.

Every day he would sport his matching Sears green pants and long-sleeve shirt and be prepared to fix a pump, climb under a tank or pass a grape lug. He was a working winemaker, who customers would at times confuse for the plumber. Eventually, Larry changed to blue work clothes to avoid confusion with George Barrington, who worked as the winery "engineer" and was legendary. George finally retired at age 85 to pursue bird watching.

A lot of the progressive social values of the 1960s were joining a new decade, along with political awareness, environmental concerns, women's liberation and gains to civil rights. Many of the winery employees and family were affectionately calling Uncle Larry "Boss" –a name I had given him while I was still in my teens doing after-school cellar work.

In the early 1970s, Larry joined forces with the Cribari brothers, classmates from his Santa Clara University days. The winery was now receiving regular bulk wine shipments from the Central Valley for the Cribari Winery. Altar wine in tanker trucks would arrive, blends were made, lab work completed and thousands of cases per month were shipped out. Many a time I stayed up all night filtering this sweet communion wine so the crew could bottle in the morning, as I dragged myself to an 8:00 A.M. class at Cabrillo College. In the fall, we juggled custom work with loads of Sylvaner grapes from Vine Hill Vineyards.

Vintage hand-corker used in the winery through the 1970s.

Typically, Monday through Friday the production crew would join in for lively discussions, and, on the weekends, Larry would join the retail staff to wind down and share the daily happenings. These gatherings also acted as informal management meetings, allowing Larry to get input for new initiatives and share concerns and expectations over operations. He was not fond of formal meetings. Pale Dry Sherry time was his way of staying connected to these dedicated employees, taking time to relax, tilting his head back and laughing heartily.

The Boss's life was cut short. But we knew that our uncle lived a life of meaning, purpose and responsibility to something greater than self.

Larry had an informal management style. At the end of each workday, he would meet the employees in the tasting room. Here with a glass of Pale Dry Sherry, served by Patti Ballard, "the Boss" would hold court. He would lead heady discussions about history, philosophy, politics and religion (St. Thomas Aquinas was a favorite). I would sit on the antique corker and listen to this rationale with some interest. I also drifted and wondered how many corks passed through the jaws of the "working relic," one arm pull at a time.

The nurturing instinct of women brings a new perspective and quality to the industry. Our attention to detail, patience and emotional stamina coincide well with the painstaking winemaking process. Women are creators and their skills can bear rich fruit. It is a satisfying lifestyle from vintage to vintage.

—*Beverly Regan Bargetto*

The Fourth Generation

Chapter Six

The Fourth Generation Takes Charge
1983-Present

Beverly Bargetto was winery president from 1982-2002.

Lawrence Bargetto was at the center of all the spokes that made the Bargetto Winery "wheel" turn. Although not a micromanager, Larry was a hands-on president and involved in all aspects of winery operations: administration, retail sales, marketing and production. With his untimely death in 1982, a huge void was created. A new leader would have to step forward. Beverly Bargetto, Larry's wife of 28 years, took the reigns of leadership at this critical juncture. Not only was Beverly deeply mourning the loss of her beloved husband, but now she was thrust into the leadership role of the winery. While familiar with winery operations on a daily basis, Beverly never had any direct business responsibilities. Living on the property, she saw all of the winery activities and she certainly was a trusted advisor to Larry. However, suddenly becoming the winery president was not something she wanted or expected. The unexpected death of "the boss" created a baptism by fire for Beverly.

In December, 1982, Beverly Bargetto became president of Bargetto Winery. She was assisted by her nephews, Tom and Jim, who continued their work in sales. Her son Martin, having completed his degree at UC Davis in viticulture, had returned to the winery in the summer of 1982, with plans to work in France. Instead, in 1983 Martin became the winery general manager. That same year, her daughter Loretta, having finished her accounting degree from the University of San Francisco, returned to operate the growing wine club with an old-fashioned Rolodex of customers. This was the pre-computer era.

During this transition, Geoff Fischer, another UC Davis enology graduate, continued as the winemaker, as he had since 1980. In 1983, a special wine and new label was released to honor Lawrence J. Bargetto, the man and vintner. The special wine was the 1981 Lawrence J. Bargetto Dedication Cabernet Sauvignon. This release received numerous accolades and gold medals. The leading wine publication, *The Wine Spectator*, placed the Dedication Cabernet in its Top Ten list of gold medal-winning Cabernet Sauvignons from the outstanding 1981 vintage. Dedicated to Larry, this wine became the centerpiece of the winery's 50th anniversary which was celebrated in 1983. Later, in 1987 the Bargetto brand was changed to Lawrence J. Bargetto.

Beverly, Martin, John, Tom, Loretta and Paul Bargetto, 1986.

1981

LAWRENCE J. BARGETTO
DEDICATION

NAPA VALLEY
CABERNET SAUVIGNON

Bargetto

PRODUCED AND BOTTLED BY BARGETTO WINERY, SOQUEL, CALIFORNIA, U.S.A. ALCOHOL 12.8% BY VOLUME

Robert Parker
93 Points

Robert M. Parker, Jr.'s
The WINE ADVOCATE
An independent consumer's bimonthly guide to Fine Wine

BARGETTO   1987 CHARDONNAY "MILLER RANCH" SANTA CRUZ MTNS.   93

50 years of good taste

BARGETTO WINERY

3535 N. Main Street   700 Cannery Row
Soquel, CA 95073   Monterey, CA
(408) 475-2258   (408) 373-4053

76

VINTAGE BARGETTO: Celebrating a Century of California Winemaking.

The label for the Dedication Cabernet Sauvignon was designed, with deep fondness for Larry, by Santa Cruz native and longtime Bargetto graphic designer Ed Penniman. Previously he had designed wine labels for Inglenook, Lejon brandy and Italian Swiss Colony wine in San Francisco prior to setting up his design office in Santa Cruz. Penniman was hired by Larry in 1972, and he played a key role at Bargetto in package design for decades. In the ensuing years, Penniman designed award-winning labels for the various brands: Santa Cruz Cellars jug wines, Bargetto, Bargetto Reserve, LA VITA, Chaucer's fruit wines and Chef Luigi vinegar.

Shortly after Larry's death, the Soquel business leaders decided to dedicate the main bridge in Soquel to Larry. This was done to recognize Larry's outstanding leadership both as a longtime businessman and as a civic leader in helping to initiate the Soquel Creek Water Board. The Water Board, founded in 1961, was led by Ken Izant of Izant's Hardware. Larry, in 1963, also directed the building of Good Shepherd Catholic School, under the leadership of Fr. Francis Markey, then pastor of St. Joseph's Church in Capitola. In 1984, John Bargetto, just 23 years old, and with the ink barely dry on his college diploma, returned to the family business and became winemaker. After generations of winemakers, John was the first in the family to earn a winemaking degree, with a degree in enology from UC Davis. From 1984-1986, John, with his cousin Paul Bargetto as cellarmaster, directed major improvements in production, including a new fermentation room, new stainless steel tanks, and a new refrigeration system (vital for controlling temperature of fermenting wines). Together John and Paul introduced barrel fermentation of Chardonnay with sur lies (aging wine on yeast after fermentation) to create a richer and more complex wine.

In 1985, John hired André Tchelistcheff as consulting winemaker. John had met him at Jordan Winery in Sonoma County during the crush of 1983 where André was a longtime consultant. André was a Russian aristocrat who had barely survived the bloody Russian Revolution; he later moved to France and then immigrated to the Napa Valley. Tchelistcheff later became the legendary winemaker at Beaulieu Vineyards in Napa from 1939-1973. He developed the Georges De Latour Private Reserve Cabernet Sauvignon. These wines were the standard for decades by which all other top

Cabernet Sauvignons in California were measured. Later in life, Tchelistcheff enjoyed consulting for young winemakers, and became known as the "dean of California winemakers." Although famous for Cabernet Sauvignon, André truly loved French Burgundies and California Pinot Noirs. John would joke with Tchelistcheff that, "together they had 75 years of winemaking experience...74 for André and 1 for John."

In 1985, John and Paul Bargetto, under Tchelistcheff's tutelage, started the winery's premier Pinot Noir program. Pinot Noir fruit from the Santa Cruz Mountains (SCM) was scarce. After many blind tastings, the winery settled on grapes from highly acclaimed Madonna Vineyard in Carneros (southern Napa). Bargetto committed to purchasing the most expensive grapes in the history of the winery at $1,500 per ton. The 1985 vintage won a Gold medal at the London International Wine Competition.

In 1986, the winery was producing Chardonnay from Tepusquet Vineyard in Santa Maria Valley. The Central Coast appellation was not well established at the time, and most premium wineries were producing expensive and heavily oaked Chardonnays. Bargetto decided to explore a new style of wine, fruity with a "kiss of oak." It was called "Cypress Chardonnay" to distinguish this wine from the richer Bargetto style Chardonnay. The name "Cypress" was in reference to the famous "lone cypress" tree in Monterey. The wine sold for $6 per bottle and was one of the few Chardonnays under $10 from a premium winery at the time. It was a hit in the market and soon became the winery's best-selling wine. (The wine name was trademarked and later sold to J. Lohr Winery.)

In 1985 the winery was still primarily a retail operation. However, a big boost came to the Cannery Row tasting room. Julie Packard, daughter of Hewlett-Packard founder William Packard, opened the Monterey Bay Aquarium, just one block from the Bargetto tasting room on Cannery Row. This new tourist attraction on the Row brought a significant increase in sales to the Bargetto tasting room for years.

Starting in 1985, with Cabernet Sauvignon from Bates Ranch in Gilroy, Martin and John together re-initiated the winery's SCM program. This followed in 1986 with Chardonnay grapes from the

John Bargetto and legendary wine-maker André Tchelistcheff in the winery laboratory in 1985.

"Consulting visits from André and wife Dorothy were always a highlight. Visits would start with a gracious light breakfast in mom's dining room, followed by full morning wine tasting in the lab...then a long lunch. I always knew how special Andre was as a friend and mentor."
—*John Bargetto*

1986

LAWRENCE J. BARGETTO

CENTRAL COAST

Cypress · Chardonnay

PRODUCED & BOTTLED BY BARGETTO WINERY, SOQUEL, CALIFORNIA, USA ALCOHOL 12.5% BY VOLUME

Miller Ranch (later known as Trout Gulch Vineyard) in Aptos.

John and Martin, realizing that the winery would need some more marketing moxie, decided that they both should continue their education. In 1986, with tears in his mother's eyes, John set off for South Bend, Indiana to earn his MBA at the University of Notre Dame. The following year Martin, while working at the winery, started his MBA program at the University of San Francisco. Paul Wofford, a Fresno State enology graduate, was hired as winemaker and led the production staff for 18 years. Wofford, having worked at Martin Ray Vineyards in the SCM, embraced the SCM vision and dedicated himself to producing outstanding wines from the region.

One of Wofford's first wines, the 1987 SCM Chardonnay, was a big hit in the wine world and got a great write up from internationally recognized Robert Parker in his publication *The Wine Advocate.* The phone rang off the hook with distributors interested in this wine. The power of the press was clear.

In 1989, with both Martin and John back from school with new ideas, they decided it was time to go national with Bargetto wines. Martin, now marketing director for the winery, led an enthusiastic team of three who set out together to build the Bargetto and Chaucer's labels as national brands. On the team were: Martin (Eastern Region), Tom (Southeast Region), John (Midwest Region) and Jim Vaughan (Western Region). Together these four traveled to "the four corners" to introduce the wines through new licensed distributors, and within years, opened 80 new wholesalers.

Years later, Tom and John laughed that the Johnny Cash song,

"I've Been Everywhere, Man" with the lyrics, "I've been everywhere, man...crossed the deserts bare, man, I've been to Sarasota, Amarillo, Nashville, Santa Fe, Little Rock, Waterloo, Boston, Trenton, Ottawa, Bakersfield..." could have been their theme. And travel they did! In the years that followed, Bargetto wines were available in nearly all 50 states and were being exported to Mexico, Canada, the Caribbean, Central America and Hong Kong. Soon winery sales reached a peak of 45, 000 cases.

At harvest time in October of 1989, the 7.0 Loma Prieta earthquake, with an epicenter just three miles from the winery, struck the San Francisco Bay Area. Some people were killed in Oakland when a section of the freeway collapsed. Injuries might have been worse, but many people were already home or at Candlestick Park in San Francisco for the "Bay Bridge" World Series. Downtown Santa Cruz was hit hard, and several people lost their lives when buildings collapsed on the Pacific Garden Mall. Bargetto Winery sustained moderate damage when several barrels fell off the racks and a tank of fermenting wine went down the drain when the stainless door came ajar. The earthquake was so powerful that tanks full of young wine weighing 20 tons partially pulled up the lag bolts from the concrete slab.

There were other "fault lines" in the winery. Controversy over the use of the Bargetto brand for both varietals and fruit wines continued to be a contentious issue within the Bargetto family. As the wine market became more crowded with new brands, and consumer attention became more limited, confusion grew about Bargetto's identity in the marketplace. Beverly Bargetto was resistant to change, continuing to hold to her husband's position that the same brand could be used for both lines. A consulting company was hired and they surveyed how Bargetto consumers viewed the winery. The results were mixed, indicating cross association of the two wine lines. The family continued to be proud of these outstanding quality fruit wines, yet confusion in the marketplace remained.

In 1990, after decades of discussion, it was finally decided that it was time to settle the re-branding issue of the fruit wines at a marketing department meeting. After a heated debate (with John going to cousin Tom's house the morning of the vote to urge a "change" vote) and a narrow vote, it was decided that the Chaucer's brand would be used for all the fruit wines. As it turned out, this was a logical move because Chaucer's Mead had become the best seller of the fruit wines, and was quickly growing in sales across the country, in retail stores and at Renaissance Fairs.

American Airlines first-class wine menu featuring Bargetto 1996 Gewurztraminer.

1986 Cabernet Savignon signed by S.F. Giants' baseball greats Willie Mays and Bobby Bonds.

Wine produced by SCM wineries as fundraiser for earthquake relief.

Progression of Bargetto Winery labels from early 1980s to the present.

Silver serving tray: Chairman's Award from Farmer's Fair Wine Competition 1983.

Wanting to expand the SCM wine program, the family was in pursuit of property for an estate vineyard. In 1991, a location on Green Valley Road in Corralitos was chosen. Once again the winery, with its own constant investment needs, was not in a position to provide funding. As former winemaker, John spearheaded this ambitious new project, and was forced to look for outside investors, as his father did years earlier. Regan Vineyards, a California Limited Partnership was established with eight outside partners. The first planting took place in May, 1992.

In 1992, Richard Bargetto, after graduating from law school and practicing law in San Jose and San Francisco, returned to the family business to start the direct mail program and provided guidance to the winery on legal issues and personnel matters.

In 1993, the U.S. wine industry reached another milestone. Consumption of fine varietal wines surpassed the consumption of bulk generic wines (like Chablis and Burgundy). It was the latest sign that the wine industry was not only growing, but also growing with sophistication. Bargetto Winery was poised for this expanding premium wine market. Looking to expand into the affordably priced "fighting varietal" (under $6 per bottle) and develop private label wines for restaurants, the winery started importing wine from Chile, Argentina and Bulgaria. Sold under the Coastal Cellars label, this project was abandoned five years later, as the winery decided to focus on premium wines.

Five years later, in 1998, the main bridge in Soquel was finally dedicated to Lawrence J. Bargetto, and his brother Ralph unveiled the new plaque. A time capsule with photos of Soquel were placed in a container which was deposited in the southeast pillar. This was done in conjunction with Soquel's sesquicentennial (150th) anniversary.

"It seems to me appropriate that this bridge be re-named in honor of a man who in so many ways, in his own life acted as a bridge builder."
—*Excerpt from May 16, 1998 bridge dedication speech by John Bargetto*

As the new millennium approached, there was great concern nationally about how computers would deal with the millennial date change of 2000. Some feared that all computers would shut down.

Beverly and "the boys," Tom, John and Martin, circa 1992.

Plaque on Bargetto Bridge
in Soquel. Photo courtesy
Gianna Bargetto.

Below Left: Suzi Rossi, winery
controller in 1999.
Below right: Michael Sones,
Bargetto winemaker.

John, Beverly and Tom Bargetto in Regan
Vineyards at the occasion of the inagural
Press Luncheon, in 1993.

Longtime employee Suzi Rossi, who started in the office in 1976 and became winery controller, took the lead on this issue for the winery. Rossi and Bargetto Winery received national TV coverage when NBC News reported on the administrative challenge Bargetto Winery encountered as it prepared for "Y2K." Suzi Rossi had been a longtime confidante to "the Boss" and was a trusted advisor to Beverly for years.

In 2001, the winery established its first advisory board with Larry Henninger from the Santa Clara University Family Business Institute and John Sheela, former President of Kenwood Vineyards. (Later, in 2010 Donna Bargetto Mohr joined her siblings on the Board.)

In the new millennium, the winery was ready to make significant investments in production. In 2001, a state-of-the-art German Europress was purchased to handle 22 tons of grapes at one time and yield finer wines. This stainless steel press with internal bladder allowed the "must" (newly crushed grapes) or newly fermented pomace to be pressed very gently, yielding juice with lower solids and less bitter tannin. A few years later, a new bottling line was installed that allowed for pressure-sensitive labels to be used, and then a new screw-capping machine was installed. In 2006, the largest tank in the history of the winery was placed adjacent to where Grandpa Bargetto had installed his 12,017 gallon redwood tank in 1949. This new 12,700 gallon tank, was not only larger, but also was made of shiny stainless steel and came with refrigeration jackets.

In 2004, Michael Sones, a UC Davis enology graduate was hired as winemaker. Sones, originally

from Brighton, England, first learned about California wines while sailing on cruise lines as a professional photographer. After graduating from UC Davis, Michael worked for leading wineries in the area, which included Ridge, David Bruce and Bonny Doon, and brought to Bargetto his diverse wine-making experience.

Having spent years working at the family winery, in 1987, cousins Peter and Paul Bargetto, along with longtime Bargetto Winery employee Jon Morgan started their own winery called Soquel Vineyards. They began their operations in the former bonded site of Grover Gulch Winery, located just up the road from Bargetto Winery. In 2002, the trio made the bold step of building a beautiful Italianate winery on Glen Haven Road. Together they purchased a five-acre piece of the original Bargetto "ranch," and even found some of Grandpa John Bargetto's old plum trees planted in the 1920s. Today, visitors enjoy sweeping views of the Monterey Bay, views that John and Philip would certainly have enjoyed nearly a century prior. On the neighboring piece, also formerly part of the original Bargetto "ranch," old vines including perhaps "old vine" Zin had been discovered.

Soquel Vineyards focuses on SCM varietals, and has built their reputation on award-winning Chardonnays and Pinot Noirs. A new family wine "scion" has been born, and Bargetto family relations remain close. In fact, Soquel Vineyards purchases grapes from Regan Vineyards and both wineries share equipment. (Paul Bargetto was one of four Bargetto family members who nearly perished in October, 2004 when an early blizzard hit Rae Lake at 10,000 feet elevation in the high Sierra. This story created national television coverage.)

In 2003, Beverly turned 79 years old, and decided it was time for her to move to the position of Board of Directors Chairperson. Martin was voted by the family to the position of president. With leadership and commitment, Martin took the reigns of the winery. Years later during the "Great Recession," when the wine industry was experiencing a downturn, Martin held firm to the tiller and navigated the winery through these challenging times.

In 2008, the winery celebrated its 75th anniversary and released its first "Old Vine" Zinfandel from Lodi in the "retro" label, which was the same label used in the 1940s.

Soquel Vineyards founders, Peter & Paul Bargetto and Jon Morgan.

12,700 gallon stainless steel tank replaced Grandpa Bargetto's 12,017 gallon redwood tank.

Gavel given as gift to Beverly Bargetto when she became Chairperson of Board.

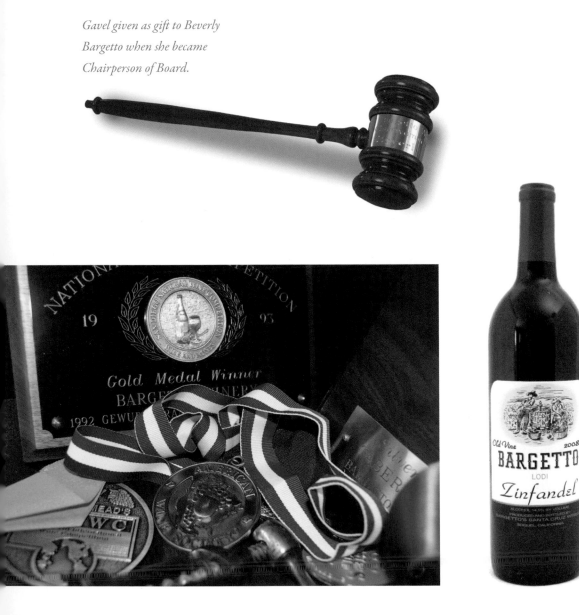

The California State Fair continued to be the leading wine competition in the wine industry. Today the family still strives to keep Larry's goal of "producing the best wine in California" alive. In recent years, with top awards, the decades of hard work are coming to fruition as evidenced by the awards.

For three summers in a row, Bargetto wines won "Best Varietal in California":

Summer 2009: Bargetto 2006 Regan Reserve Merlot
"Best in California"
Summer 2010: Bargetto 2007 Regan Reserve Pinot Noir
"Best in California"
Summer 2011: LA VITA 2008
"Best Italian varietal blend wine in California"

During a period of several years, the winery expanded and upgraded the retail operations. These improvements have allowed the winery to host many events like weddings, private parties and fundraisers for the community. This beautiful setting, overlooking Soquel Creek, plays host to music series and art shows.

In 2012, family members voted for Loretta Bargetto to become president. Loretta leads the fourth generation of SCM winemakers in its never-ending pursuit of producing world class Santa Cruz Mountains wines.

In January of 2013, Bargetto Winery reached its 80th anniversary year, and scheduled numerous events to celebrate the milestone. Beverly, although failing in health, lived long enough to see the winery's 80th anniversary year. In her time, she provided vital leadership and oversaw a transition to the next generation of Bargettos. Beverly left the winery in a much better place than she found it. Walking the winery property in her last days, Beverly seemed to be reminding all that she would still be watching over things for many years to come.

Sadly, on January 14, 2013 Beverly died peacefully at home on the winery property. For nearly 60 years, Beverly, a fine Irish lady from San Francisco, who moved to Soquel in 1954 to marry Larry, had integrated well into the Italian enclave. With her strength and grace, she left her mark on the family, winery and community. She will not be forgotten.

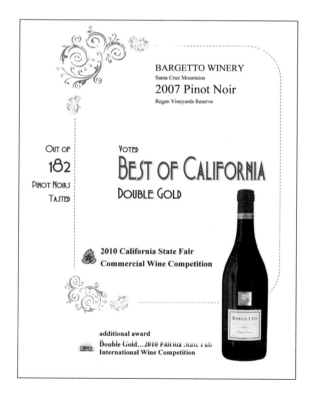

BARGETTO WINERY
Santa Cruz Mountains
2007 Pinot Noir
Regan Vineyards Reserve

OUT OF
182
PINOT NOIRS
TASTED

VOTED
BEST OF CALIFORNIA
DOUBLE GOLD

2010 California State Fair Commercial Wine Competition

additional award
Double Gold...2010 Florida State Fair International Wine Competition

Beverly (middle) with her five children, Martin, Loretta, Richard, John and Donna under the creekside sycamore tree in 2002.

Until one is committed, there is hesitancy, the chance to draw back... the moment one commits oneself, then providence moves, too...Whatever you can do or dream you can do, begin it! Boldness has genius, power and magic in it. Begin it now!

—Based on quote from Goethe (1749-1832)

Regan Vineyards

Chapter Seven

Regan Vineyards, LA VITA is born

For decades, the conversation around the Bargetto family dinner table would inevitably turn to the same topic...the need for a Santa Cruz Mountains (SCM) vineyard. Only with a substantial vineyard could the family realize its dream of a full-fledged Santa Cruz Mountains wine program. In 1973, "the Boss," Larry Bargetto, came close to realizing his vision of establishing a large vineyard, but the deal fell through at the last moment when the financier backed out.

In 1988, now back from graduate school, John Bargetto and his mother Beverly took up the mission to establish a SCM vineyard. John and Beverly traveled all over Santa Cruz County searching for a suitable piece of property on which to plant the dream vineyard. They hunted from Boulder Creek to Bonny Doon, from the hills of Soquel and Aptos, to the open farmland of sunny Corralitos.

Wanting to systematically evaluate each potential piece of property, John devised a system of five "S's" as parameters to rate and record each piece of land. The five were: Sun (exposure), Slope (how steep), Soil (quality), Street (accessibility), and Sales Price (cost per acre). "We hiked a lot of steep goat trails," John described. They soon learned that smaller parcels of land competed with the expensive housing market, thereby making those less expansive plots economically unfeasible. They soon realized that they needed something larger.

By this time, the boundaries of the SCM appellation were well established. The lines followed elevation contours of the rolling hills. On the western side, facing the Pacific Ocean, the line followed the 400-foot elevation contour. With a few exceptions, the eastern boundary followed the 800 foot contour line of the Santa Cruz Mountains and overlooked the warmer Santa Clara Valley.

In the summer of 1991, John and Beverly settled on a 50-acre piece of property in Corralitos, which was planted to apple trees. It was beautiful property with rolling hills, rich alluvial soil and a stunning view of the Monterey Bay. There was something that just felt right about this property and the family agreed to buy it.

With John as managing general partner, a California Limited Partnership was formed, which pro-

Regan Vineyards overlooking the Monterey Bay, photo courtesy Michael Sones.

LA VITA photo courtesy Ed Penniman.

*In 2001 a gazebo was built
to host visitors.*

vided the necessary structure and financing to both purchase the property and to plant grapevines. John convinced Beverly to sell a half acre of the original Bargetto Winery property to provide the down payment on the new vineyard. John promised her that he would turn those few "dirt clods" into a beautiful estate and call it Regan Vineyards, Beverly's maiden name. Anxious to plant in the spring of 1992, vines were ordered. John knew this was risky, recalling his father had done the same thing. Would he, too, have to sell vines from the winery parking lot as his father had done, if the deal was not completed?

While in escrow, Alfred Conde, the co-owner (along with Gilbert Mello) of the land dropped a bombshell, with an innocuous question, "John, you do know that this is the same piece of property that your father almost purchased years ago?" The question hit John like a lightning bolt! After searching all over the vast SCM range, what was the chance that the family would choose the very same property, unbeknownst to them, that Larry was poised to purchase nearly 20 years earlier? Sweet destiny seemed to have settled upon this unique land. Beverly was thrilled with the news, knowing that she was able to carry out her husband's vision on the very same piece of property! That winter, John, while walking an area of the new vineyard, with clay soil sticking to his boots, suddenly realized that this was indeed the same piece that he had walked as a young boy with his father.

Professor William "Jack" Regan, first cousin to Beverly and longtime business advisor to Larry, was the first limited partner to sign up. Seven additional limited partners were eventually added, including Bernie Turgeon. Turgeon was the former co-owner of Turgeon and Lohr Winery (later J. Lohr Winery). By 1992, Bernie was owner of Trout Gulch Vineyards (formerly Miller Ranch) in Aptos, from where Bargetto Winery had purchased grapes for years.

Prior to planting, the vineyard soil had to be prepared. Steve Malatesta of Watsonville was hired to "rip" the dirt deeply with three-foot-long shanks to break up the hard pan layer of topsoil. This practice allowed for fumigation of the soil to kill root-knot nematodes that were identified in the soil. (These were the same worm-like pests that fed on vine roots and killed the vineyard next to the winery in the 1970s.) The ripping also gave the young plant roots full opportunity to grow. One added benefit to fumigation was that it temporarily killed the gopher population. In time, these root-eating varmints would prove to be the most serious pest at Regan Vineyards.

The first planting of 10 acres of Chardonnay took place in May of 1992 and included more than 50 enthusiastic family and friends. These "weekend warriors" worked on their hands and knees for a full day planting the vines, filling the holes, installing milk cartons around the plants for protection from deer, and hooking up drip irrigation lines.

Knowing the unique quality of the Mt. Eden clone of Chardonnay that harkened back to early SCM vintner Paul Masson, four acres of this clone were planted at Regan. The remaining six acres of Section 1 was planted to Clone 4, a traditional clone of Chardonnay found in Napa and Sonoma.

By the early 1990s, Merlot was the "hot" wine in California, with raging popularity nationwide. Although Merlot had traditionally been planted in warmer sites next to Cabernet Sauvignon, it was decided to pioneer Merlot at Regan, which was located less than seven miles from the cool water of the Monterey Bay. It is widely known that Merlot thrives in Bordeaux, France, which is a cool Region 2 (back to UC Davis's Winkler); and one of the world's most famous Merlot-based wines, Chateau Petrus, comes from Bordeaux, so it seemed Merlot could do well at Regan. In winter of 1993, with encouragement from cousin Tom Bargetto, John decided to plant Merlot in the heavier, alluvial soil of the eastern side of the property. The vines thrived, and in time yielded powerful wines, deep in color and rich in fruit.

It was clear that Pinot Noir would be a natural match for this cool-climate Regan site. The challenge was to choose which clones of Pinot Noir would be best. A clone is a genetic mutation of a variety, and especially with Pinot Noir, various clones can yield vastly different wine.

At this time, there were dozens of clones of Pinot Noir, with many new clones emerging on the viticulture scene. John attended a technical tasting at UC Davis, and traveled to Oregon to conduct research. In addition, he talked to many experienced winegrowers, like Richard "Dick" Graff of Chalone Vineyard (Monterey County). Eventually it was decided that three clones would be planted: Pommard (which was widely and successfully planted in Oregon), Dijon 115 (a new clone arriving on the wine scene), and the Martini clone (a classic California clone named after Louis Martini in Napa). (Years later the Mt. Eden clone of Pinot Noir would prove to be superior.)

From the onset of the vineyard project, the family wanted to grow Italian varietals in keeping with

Beverly Bargetto planting a dormant Merlot vine.

Young Chardonnay vines growing.

Chardonnay clusters at harvest.
Photo courtesy Ed Penniman

the Bargetto Italian heritage established by generations of Bargetto family winemakers. After all, by this time the Bargettos had been part of the California wine industry for one hundred years, going back to Giuseppe and Filippo at Casa Delmas in 1890. The plan at Regan was to have an Italian white wine and an Italian red wine.

The choice of Italian white was relatively simple–the classic Italian white, Pinot Grigio, fruity, light and refreshing. *Perfetto!* In 1993, Bargetto Winery started producing Pinot Grigio (literally "gray" Pinot in Italian) from grapes grown in Santa Barbara County. At the time, boatloads of Pinot Grigio were consumed in the U.S., either from inexpensive Italian-made wine, or Pinot Gris (same varietal) from Oregon. The Pinot Grigio craze in California was still a decade away. In fact, at the time the Regan Pinot Grigio vines were ordered in 1993, there were only 66 planted acres in all of California, as recorded by the California Grape Crush Report. Little did the Bargettos know that in a few short years, Pinot Grigio would become the hottest wine in American markets, second only to Chardonnay in U.S. consumption.

At the same time that the Pinot Grigio vines were ordered, the Regan Italian red wine was to be decided. The family's vision was to produce a unique northern Italian red blended wine, one that had never before been produced. This was no easy task, as anyone who travels to Italy knows of the many wines there, not to mention all the Italian wines produced in California. Blending is a vital aspect of winemaking, and there is something "magical" about a three-wine blend. The first two red varietals chosen for Regan were Nebbiolo (Lampia and Michete clones), the great wine of

Piemonte, that yields the world famous Barolo (like Gaja), and Dolcetto, the intense fruity variety from the Bargetto home town of Castelnuovo Don Bosco.

Yet, this unique blended wine (still unnamed) would require a third varietal. Barbera was rejected as having too much acidity, and Nebbiolo already had plenty. Charbono was chosen, until it was discovered that, although having an Italian name in California, it is a French variety.

Once again UC Davis came to the rescue. While John was attending a technical class on California Italian varietals, a little known wine named Refosco was tasted. It had a distinct peppery aroma, and was deep in color. (According to reports at the seminar, August Sebastiani used to plant it in his vineyard to add color to the wines.) Voila! The three varieties were chosen to create this new wine. The dormant plants arrived in winter of 1995, in the middle of a winter flood. (This time Soquel was spared, and instead the Pajaro River jumped its banks and caused damage to south county in the Watsonville area.) The Italian vines were planted in the most shallow hillside soil at Regan, in an attempt to restrain the vigor of these Italian vines.

Prior to Regan, Alfred Conde had farmed the property since the 1960s with apples. From the inception of Regan until 1998, Conde was the vineyard foreman. Conde, the experienced farmer, worked hard and brought his vast background to the project. For years, Conde rose early in the morning while it was still dark and sprayed the vineyard for disease control when the wind was calm. Conde, the veteran farmer and limited partner, and John, the winemaker and "college kid" general partner were an interesting duo, yet they worked together with a common vision to establish a beautiful and productive vineyard.

One sweet family story about the new vineyard reflects the joy and sense of adventure involved in the new endeavor. During dinner one evening at the Bargetto home, John had been telling his wife, Sharon, and three young kids about how barn owl boxes had been installed in the vineyard, and they had recently spotted the first owls.

Just then, the phone rang, Sharon answered and said, "John, Al is on

The first Regan Vineyards wine was the 1996 Chardonnay.

"Unfiltered Reserve" Merlot from the 1997 blockbuster "vintage of the century."

the phone," handing the phone to John. Three-year-old Kevin's eyes opened wide and in amazement, mistaking the name of the vineyard foreman for the nocturnal raptor, turned to his sister, and yelped, "Nini (short for Gianna), the owl has a telephone!"

In 1997, there were just 18 fully productive acres at Regan. The Chardonnay was in its sixth leaf (sixth growing season), the Merlot was in its fifth leaf, and the Italian varietals and Pinot Noir section was yielding its first small harvest. The spring was warm and pleasant, the plants set a large crop, and the summer was warm, and Regan, along with the rest of California, experienced the "vintage of the century." Grape demand and prices were high, especially for Merlot. The vines yielded a record humongous 194 tons, the biggest ever at Regan, and the wines were astonishingly wonderful. The winegrowers, wineries and consumers were all rewarded! The Bargetto Reserve Merlot won two gold medals, including one at the *Dallas Morning News Competition.*

In 1999, with demand for Merlot wine and grapes still high (the *Sideways* movie still unreleased), and with the success of the 1997 vintage still fresh, the winery was in need of more Merlot, so the final six acres at Regan were planted to this popular variety This time, a new trellis system, known as lyre, was utilized, one that would better handle the vigorous growth of the Merlot vines.

The lyre system is a "double vertical" system in which the shoots are trained to grow in two vertical "walls," with a divided vine canopy about three feet apart. Although more expensive with its 12 wires, the lyre system offers many advantages. Shoots are trained upwards, away from the clusters to allow more sunlight directly on the grape clusters. With better exposed grapes, the wines have more color and flavor, and less "green" aromas. This system also helps with disease control of mildew and botrytis, because the increased sunlight and airflow decrease disease pressure. This is

2006 LA VITA won best "Italian Varietal Blend" in California, at the California State Fair.

The 2001 LA VITA label, featuring cubist artist Juan Gris, won "Best of Show" from 3,500 labels at the Orange County Fair.

Left to right:
Jack Regan, Beverly and John Bargetto
and Beth Svee of the
Porter Memorial Public Library.

Vintage	Beneficiary
1997	Jacob's Heart
1998	Siena Maternity House
1999	Hospice Caring Project
2000	Santa Cruz Search and Rescue
2001	Good Shepherd Catholic School
2002	St. Francis Soup Kitchen
2003	Porter Memorial Public Library
2004	Santa Cruz Ballet Theatre
2006	CASA of Santa Cruz County
2007	Watsonville YMCA
2008	Shakespeare Santa Cruz
2009	Santa Cruz Art League

particularly important in foggy areas along the coast.

The first harvest of grapes from the LA VITA varieties came during the great 1997 vintage. Four years later, in 2001, it was time to release the inaugural wine. For years, the family and marketing people at the winery searched for a proprietary wine name that could be used for this unique wine. A name contest was even held with lots of names considered. At the time, many wineries in California were using proprietary names like Tapestry (BV), Opus One (Robert Mondavi) or Siena (Ferrari-Carano). Initially, the family considered VINUM (wine in Latin). Instead the name LA VITA was chosen, meaning 'Life" in Italian to reflect how wine brings so much vitality, richness and joy to our world.

For this distinct wine, John initially envisioned an art series label, one that would feature famous lovers of wine down through the ages, e.g., poets, presidents (Thomas Jefferson), artists (Caravaggio) and musicians (Vivaldi). The concept was that the label would change each year. The label series eventually evolved to "Art in Wine," to showcase the artists' work on the label. LA VITA would feature how artists have included wine in artwork since the dawn of civilization, from ancient Egyptians to modern-day artists. John corroborated with graphic designer Ed Penniman on the design of each year's label.

In May, 2001, the inaugural LA VITA wine from the 1997 vintage was released to rave reviews. The wine was priced at $50 bottle, and was considered Bargetto Winery's finest effort to date. The first vintage of LA VITA won four gold medals, and the 1998 vintage that followed won a gold medal at the *San Francisco Chronicle Wine Competition* and Best of Class award at the California State Fair. The 2006 vintage, produced under the leadership of winemaker Michael Sones, won the coveted "Best Italian Blend" award from the California State Fair.

In addition to the unique blend and art series label, the final dimension of LA VITA was the commitment from the winery to use this wine as a vehicle to make a contribution back to the Santa Cruz community in a more formal way. Thus, each year a nonprofit organization in Santa Cruz County is chosen to receive cash and wine from the proceeds of LA VITA. Each organization receives special attention at the annual release party. It is the Bargetto family's way of saying *thank you* to the Santa Cruz community, one that has been so supportive of the winery in Soquel for three generations.

By 1999, all of the Regan property was planted to vines. It was now time to have a place to host

Kevin, Elisa and Gianna Bargetto on the new Regan tractor, Christmas 1998.

visitors, winery employees, partners and the wine press. Not wanting to use vital vineyard property and looking for a good view, a gazebo (with seed money from Uncle Jack Regan and his wife Liz) was built on top of the existing 20,000-gallon concrete water tank with a stunning 360-degree view of the Santa Cruz Mountains, the Santa Lucia Highlands and the Monterey Bay.

Two generations after Italian-born Vittorio Zoppi ran the Bargetto "ranch" in Soquel, Jesus Figueroa from Colima, Mexico, would operate Regan Vineyards. For 14 years, Figueroa, starting in 1999, has been the Regan foreman. With tremendous devotion and hard work, Figueroa has become a leading vineyardist in the area. In time, almost all of the hardworking Hispanic workers from Mexico at the vineyard are either related to Figueroa or know him personally. Figueroa's smiling face always reminds visitors of the joy and pride that he takes in his work vintage to vintage.

Most farmers, naturally, are environmentalists. Their work keeps them close to Mother Nature, and they have an innate appreciation for the delicate systems involved in agriculture, and the scarce resources required–like water–to produce quality products.

Since its inception, Regan Vineyards (in addition to Bargetto Winery) has strived to integrate sustainable winegrowing practices in all aspects of its operation. Participating in the Wine Institute's *Code of Sustainable Winegrowing Practices*, Regan was able to evaluate how it could improve its practices. To-

Crimson clover is planted in the vine rows to host beneficial insects and add beauty to the vineyard.

Solar power creates clean renewable energy at Regan which is used for pumping the well water.

Regan Vineyards foreman Jesus Figueroa spreading compost.

Barn owls keep a watchful eye on the gopher population at Regan.

In 2010 Bargetto family won the "Farmer of the Year" award for Santa Cruz County.

Farm Bureau honors Bargettos

United States Senate

Certificate of Commendation

is hereby presented by

Dianne Feinstein,

United States Senator from California,

to

The Bargetto Family

Certificate of Special Congressional Recognition

Presented to

The Bargetto Family
2010 Farmer of the Year

in recognition of outstanding and invaluable service to the community.

June 24, 2010
DATE

MEMBER OF CONGRESS

day at Regan a full range of sustainable practices is employed, including biological control of gophers, solar panels and the use of compost.

Gophers are the biggest pests at Regan. With 30 steel traps, jokingly named the "armored division," these pests are kept in check. In addition, natural gopher control is utilized with the use of barn owls. Barn owls are nocturnal, as are gophers—a match made in heaven! Two barn owl boxes provide "free housing" for these raptors, which stealthily fly every night for evening "snacks."

Soil health is critical for vine health. In recent years, there is much greater understanding about the need for "live" dirt, as opposed to "dead" dirt. Soil that has microorganisms helps with water penetra-

Some of the third, fourth and fifth generations of the Bargetto SCM winemaking family.

tion, and assists in the release of nutrients for vine roots. Each year, truckloads of mushroom compost are spread out into the vine rows.

In 2005, Regan was one of the first vineyards in the region to install photovoltaic (PV) solar panels. The panels create clean electrical energy, which is used for pumping water from the Regan well. The Regan solar system is tied into the PG&E grid. Irrigations are timed in the morning, when electricity is inexpensive. In the afternoons, Regan "sells" electricity to PG&E at four times the rate that is paid. After a seven-year investment, the system has now paid for itself.

Starting in 1979, the Santa Cruz County Farm Bureau, under the leadership of Jess Brown, has recognized a "Farmer of the Year." In 2010, because of its long-standing history in the county, sustainable practices, and years of supporting the local community—especially through the LA VITA program— the Bargetto family was honored with the distinguished "Farmer of the Year" award.

Like Giuseppe, Filippo and Giovanni Bargetto years earlier, the Bargetto family today remains committed to producing truly outstanding wines from the Santa Cruz Mountains. The family strives to be a leader in sustainable practices, especially when resources are becoming evermore scarce. The winery commits itself to being a good "citizen" by giving back to our community through the LA VITA wine program and other ways.

The Bargetto family invites you to visit the winery in Soquel, where recently the new LA VITA room was built overlooking Soquel Creek. All the tight, vertical grain redwood in the room, originally from old-growth trees, came from the historic tanks installed by Grandpa Bargetto and his sons in the 1940s. You can taste the recent vintages, like the SCM Pinot Noir and Chardonnay, and reflect on the long legacy of Bargetto winemaking.

We hope that when you have a glass of Bargetto wine in the future, you will be able to better understand our family history and long legacy of wine in California. Perhaps you will enjoy the wine a little more, knowing that generations of hard work and experience have gone into creating that glass of wine. While you enjoy the wine, pehaps with a meal, take the time to share your own family stories with each other.

From our generation to yours, we close this story for now with a robust SALUTE!

Soquel Creek is a lovely year-round stream that tumbles down the southern flank of the Santa Cruz Mountains, cutting through some softer, rounded mid-level hills before flattening out for its final journey to the sea. John Bargetto and Geoffrey Dunn, the authors of this delightful and important history, grew up on the banks of that stream. My introduction to the name Bargetto came during winters in the 1950s while steelhead fishing in the creek.

Fishermen, like surfers, have their own nomenclature to describe streams, and the Soquel Creek was dotted with a number of Italian names for fishing holes, including Casalegno's and Bargetto's. I didn't realize it during those oh-so-cold (and usually fishless) winter mornings, but those place names, strung along the creek like rosary beads, were waiting for someone to caress them and bring forth their stories. John and Geoffrey have done just that.

The Bargetto story is a classic of what we historians call the "new" American immigration of the 1890s. And, like most immigrant stories, the Bargetto saga is one of serendipity, luck and back-breaking hard work. A map beginning with their Italian origins, and then the zigging and zagging from New York, to San Francisco, the Santa Clara Valley and, finally, to the banks of the Soquel, would resemble the very grapevines that came to symbolize the surname Bargetto.

Once secure in their new home, the Bargettos became active participants in the economics and politics of their adopted homeland. In December of 1955, the usually benign stream caused the worst flood in Soquel's recorded history. Lawrence (Larry) Bargetto was a major player in the resulting flood control efforts and was one of the founding directors of the Soquel Creek Water District, a position he held for more than 20 years.

Most of the thousands of folks who travel along Soquel Drive every day don't realize that the slightly arched bridge that spans Soquel Creek was named for Larry Bargetto in 1998. The bridge is a fitting recognition of not only his contributions to the community, but also for the entire Bargetto family presence in the valley over the past century.

Today, the names Soquel and Bargetto are synonymous. John and Geoffrey have shared with us all how that came to be. It is a remarkable story. We'll never take that bridge—or that wine—for granted again.

Afterword

From Italy to Soquel: The Grapevine of History

Sandy Lydon
Historian Emeritus,
Cabrillo College

Bibliography

Bargetto, Sylvia and Adeline.
Bargetto Family Historical Notes.
Santa Cruz/Soquel: Unpublished, 1975.

Bargetto, Ralph.
Bargetto Family Stories as Recounted by Family Members.
Soquel: Unpublished.

Dunn, Geoffrey.
Santa Cruz Is in the Heart:
Selected Writings on Local History, Culture, Politics & Ghosts.
Capitola: Capitola Book Company, 1989.

Elliott, Wallace W.
History of Santa Cruz County, California.
San Francisco: Wallace W. Elliott and Company, 1879.

Francis, Phil.
Beautiful Santa Cruz County.
San Francisco: H. S. Crocker Company, 1896.

Harrison, Edward S.
History of Santa Cruz County, California.
San Francisco: Pacific Press Publishing Company, 1892.

Holland, Michael R.
Late Harvest: The Wine History of the Santa Cruz Mountains.
Santa Cruz: The Late Harvest Project, 1983.

Lydon, Sandy and Swift, Carolyn.
Soquel Landing to Capitola-by-the-Sea.
De Anza College, 1978.

Lydon, Sandy.
Chinese Gold: The Chinese in the Monterey Bay Region
—20th Anniversary Edition.
Capitola: Capitola Book Company, 2008.

Santa Cruz Sentinel:
1880 to 1995 (Microfilm).
McHenry Library, University of California, Santa Cruz.

Street, Richard Steven.
Beasts of the Field: A Narrative History of California Farm Workers, 1769-1913.
Palo Alto: Stanford University Press, 2004.

Sullivan, Charles L.
A Companion to California Wine: An Encyclopedia of Wine and Winemaking
from the Mission Period to the Present. With a Foreword by Hugh Johnson.
Berkeley: University of California Press, 1998.

Sullivan, Charles L.
Like Modern Edens: Winegrowing in the Santa Clara Valley
and Santa Cruz Mountains.
Cupertino: California History Center, 1982.

Sullivan, Charles L., editor,
Wines and Winemakers of the Santa Cruz Mountains: An Oral History.
D.R. Bennion Trust, 1994.

Swift, Carolyn, et al., Soquel Pioneer and Historical Association.
Images of America: Soquel.
Chicago: Arcadia (Tempus), 2011.

Salesian Sisters, followers of Saint John Bosco of Castelnuovo D'Asti, in 1976 founded a school just a few miles from Regan Vineyards.

Photo courtesy John Bargetto